My Kids Are Trying to Kill Me

Words of Encouragement for Parents

Jennifer Mittelstet

WestBow
PRESS
A DIVISION OF THOMAS NELSON
& ZONDERVAN

Scriptures taken from the Holy Bible, New International Version®, NIV®.
Copyright © 1973, 1978, 1984, 2011 by Biblica, Inc.™ Used by permission of
Zondervan. All rights reserved worldwide. www.zondervan.com The "NIV"
and "New International Version" are trademarks registered in the United
States Patent and Trademark Office by Biblica, Inc.™ All rights reserved.

Scripture quotations taken from the Holy Bible, New Living Translation,
copyright 1996, 2004. Used by permission of Tyndale House
Publishers, Inc., Wheaton, Illinois 60189. All rights reserved.

All Scripture quotations in this publications are from **The Message**.
Copyright (c) by Eugene H. Peterson 1993, 1994, 1995, 1996, 2000,
2001, 2002. Used by permission of NavPress Publishing Group.

WestBow Press books may be ordered through booksellers or by contacting:
WestBow Press
A Division of Thomas Nelson & Zondervan
1663 Liberty Drive
Bloomington, IN 47403
www.westbowpress.com
1 (866) 928-1240

ISBN: 978-1-4908-2534-2 (sc)
ISBN: 978-1-4908-2536-6 (hc)
ISBN: 978-1-4908-2535-9 (e)

Library of Congress Control Number: 2014902041

Printed in the United States of America.

WestBow Press rev. date: 02/13/2014

Contents

This book is dedicated to my amazing husband and best friend. You are truly the greatest blessing God has ever given me, and I am so thankful for your love, support, and godly leadership over our family every single day.

I also dedicate this book to my three crazy boys. You are all the light of my life. I can't imagine my life without each one of you. You all bring such joy to our household, you keep us young, and you keep life interesting! I thank God each day for all three of you.

Finally, I dedicate this book to my family: my mom, who has been a constant encourager and my biggest fan throughout my life; my dad, who has always taught me to laugh at myself and never take myself too seriously; and my sister, who supports me, loves me, and stands by my side always and forever. I am so very blessed to have each of you in my life.

Foreword

I wake up each morning and thank the Lord for the blessings of my wonderful family. In all things large and small, they make me proud each and every day! On this particular day, though, I am especially proud of *my* "baby girl," Jennifer!

I think back on Jennifer as a little girl, and to this day I can clearly hear the words coming out of her mouth: "Mom, I don't ever want to have kids—they are just too much trouble."

When Jennifer and Matt announced they were pregnant for the first time, that thought came back into my mind, as I wondered how she would handle parenthood. As any first-time mom, Jennifer had to quickly learn she was no longer the "baby" of the family; she was now completely responsible for and was everything to this tiny life God had given her.

It has now been seven years and two more little gifts from God later, and I can honestly say I have never seen a more amazing mother than Jennifer! She is wise beyond her years, and as I can attest, you can teach an old dog new tricks because I learn from her every day!

I'm her mom, so you might think I'm just a wee bit biased—and maybe I am. But my hope is that you will enjoy Jennifer's story, and if anything, you will come away knowing that as a parent you are not alone in the multitude of feelings, stresses, and joys of raising children. It's truly the hardest job you will ever do in your entire life … and the most rewarding!

Claire Harmon

Introduction

I am a mom of three young boys, ages one, four, and six. They are wild, full of energy, and completely crazy! I often picture God sitting up in heaven laughing at the fact that he gave me three boys. I used to be sane, but then I had kids and I've completely lost my mind! My life is utter chaos most of the time, but I have learned so much since becoming a mom. I am *not* a parenting expert by any stretch of the imagination. Parenting feels like a learn-as-you-go kind of job. Some days it feels like I've been thrown to the wolves (as I lovingly call my boys) and have to learn to survive!

I recently quit my job to stay home with my boys. Prior to being a stay-at-home mom, I was a working mom. I taught reading and English and led the dyslexia program in middle school for seven years. So in addition to being a mom, I have worked with a lot of kids over the years. Having taught middle school, I learned that kids of all ages are basically the same. My middle school kids were just older versions of my kids. They still act silly, and they whine, argue, talk back, and disobey.

This book is completely honest and straight from my heart. There are situations that I am embarrassed to claim as my own. But if my experiences help even one person, then I am so thankful to be able to share them. God placed this book on my heart so that I can reach out and encourage other parents, as I have needed encouragement almost every day in this parenting journey. My hope is that as you read this book, you can relate, gain new perspective, and have hope for better days as a parent.

Let me tell you a little about each of my boys since I'll be referencing them throughout this book. My oldest son is Luke, and he is the six-year-old. He has more energy than any child should be allowed to have. I have compared him to other boys his age, and I am convinced there is no other child with that much energy. His preschool teacher once said to me, "I've been teaching for thirty years, and I've never taught a child with that much energy." My only thought was, *Lucky me!* In addition to his excessive amount of energy, he is also a natural-born leader. And by leader, I mean bossy and stubborn! That same preschool teacher described him this way on one of his report cards: "He's a natural leader. He just sometimes seems to lead the other kids in the wrong direction." Again, my only thought was, *Lucky me!* Luke is highly intelligent. He reasons far above his age and is quite a joy to have a conversation with. Most of the time he is so smart that he is ten steps ahead of me when we're having a conversation. And Luke has a huge heart. He cares so deeply about others and truly seeks to be a peacemaker—except with his brothers, of course! Overall, he's a really good kid, and he loves to be a big helper. I don't know what my life would be like without him.

My middle child, Eli, is four years old. If ever I could picture my dad as a young child, Eli would be him. He doesn't have a serious bone in his body, nor does my dad. He truly lives to make us laugh each day. When he does something that makes you laugh, he'll do it fifty more times just to keep you laughing. Also like my dad, he regularly embellishes when telling stories. For example, it was generally not Eli who messed up his bedroom, it was a giant man-eating dinosaur who jumped in through the window looking for a little boy to eat. You get the picture.

In addition, Eli can be quite a little stinker. Consequences don't seem to work on him. If you give him a timeout, he'll ask you to double it. If you take a toy away, he'll tell you he didn't like that toy anyway. We created some jars in our house to help us with the boys' behavior. The first jar was a treat jar. If the boys went an entire day with no consequences for bad behavior, they could draw from the treat jar. Some of the treats included getting an extra bedtime story, getting a glass of juice with lunch, staying up fifteen minutes past bedtime, etc. The other jar was the consequence jar. When the boys did something wrong, they would have to draw a consequence, including losing a toy, running five laps around the backyard, sitting in a timeout, etc. Eli is absolutely *not* motivated by these jars. One day, early on into having these jars, he drew from the consequence jar twelve times. He only earned about four or five consequences, but every time he drew a consequence, he asked for another one. He would simply state, "That wasn't so bad," each time he completed a consequence. This went on for quite some time, so we lovingly named him "Captain Consequence," a name he wears proudly.

And our youngest son, Logan, is just now coming into his little personality. He is one, and he has truly completed our family. He is a typical third child, as I pictured a third child to be. He mostly just goes with the flow and fits right in with the family schedule. He has a very laid-back, goofy personality. He loves to laugh. His favorite games are the typical games kids his age like to play: peek-a-boo and fetch (you know, where he throws his sippy cup, food, and toys, and I repeatedly go pick them up and give them back). But when he decides he wants something, you'd better watch out. He knows what he wants, and he is not easily deterred when he's on a mission. We had to take baby-proofing to a whole new level when this child was born! He has also earned a nice little nickname: "Captain Unhelpful." This child can dismantle, unload, or tear apart anything in a matter of seconds. I will walk into another room for less than a minute, and when I return, I'll often find an entire drawer or cabinet emptied out onto the floor, the dishwasher completely unloaded, or any number of things dismantled and lying in pieces on the floor. Every single time, I find him in the center of the mess with the biggest smile on his face, like he could not be more proud of his little accomplishment.

Throughout my journey as a mom, I have been so blessed to be surrounded by friends and family who have encouraged me, supported me, and given godly advice to help me. This book is a compilation of the things I have learned the hard way and the things I have gathered from those friends and family surrounding me.

It is my hope that this book brings you joy and laughter. I truly feel that life would not be complete without laughing every single day. Without laughter, I know my level of stress would be tremendous. If you can laugh at yourself, I believe you can survive anything. I also hope this book gives you some good advice that will help you on your journey as a parent, so you don't have to learn everything the hard way. But most importantly, I hope this book brings you encouragement to push through the difficult days of parenthood. Children are a true blessing and joy, but it certainly doesn't feel like that every day. Many, many days I have wondered, *What in the world was I thinking having kids?* My hope is that this book helps you to realize that you are not alone in your feelings as a parent.

My mom, the wisest person I know, tells me almost daily that being a mom is the hardest job you'll ever do. But she always follows it up by saying that it is also the most rewarding. I'm not sure I believe the second part just yet, but she's definitely right about the first part! In all seriousness, I know with all my heart that God places children in our lives to challenge us, teach us, and shape us into the people he wants us to be.

In this book, I have outlined the top things I have learned so far as a parent. These are things I believe will truly help as you learn to become a better parent every day. I'm not promising these things will make you perfect. But if you strive to focus on even some of these things, you will grow into a great parent, and your kids will be so blessed to live in a home where they are loved, cherished, and have the opportunity to grow into amazing adults.

Chapter 1

Put God First

*Be still, and know that I am God! I will be honored by
every nation. I will be honored throughout the world.*
—Psalm 46:10 (New Living Translation)

The absolute only way to survive parenthood is to rely on God
for everything every single day. My husband and I begin almost
every day on our knees, praying to God. We pray for each of our boys'
very specific daily needs. We also pray throughout the day to ask
God to help us, guide us, and give us the wisdom we need to make
it through the hours. A lot of days, it is an hour-by-hour struggle,
yet I know I can count on my God to get me through these times,
especially when I feel like there is no way I can do it on my own.

When Eli, our middle child, was around four weeks old, I really
struggled with postpartum depression, extreme exhaustion, learning
how to cope with a newborn, and his brother, Luke, twenty-three
months. To say I struggled is probably an understatement. My
husband worked long days. He left the house before the kids awoke
and arrived home most nights after they were in bed. I worked full-
time as well, just trying my hardest to survive.

One particularly difficult day, Eli cried and cried. Nothing I
tried worked. He was inconsolable. Meanwhile, Luke was running

around the house, being his normal, destructive almost-two-year-old self, and acting like a crazy person. I had lost all control of the situation—and even worse, I had lost all hope. So I did the only thing I knew how to do. I sat down and started to cry. The crying quickly turned into sobbing. Very productive, right? I thought, *What have I gotten myself into? I can't do this.* I felt exhausted and overwhelmed, and I didn't see my situation improving anytime in the near future.

At that moment, when I felt like I was at my lowest point and helpless, my precious son Luke walked up to me and forcefully hit me with a hardcover book. *Really? Was that necessary?* I cried out to God through my sobs, "Did you seriously just let that happen?"

As I was calling out to God in frustration and anger, I looked down at the book my son had used to hit me over the head. It was his Bible. In that moment my tears turned into hysterical laughter. *Okay, God, I get it! You don't actually have to hit me over the head with the Bible. Isn't that just a figure of speech, anyway? I'll read your Word when I feel like I can't press forward.*

God uses bizarre (and quite often comical) experiences to get my attention and remind me of what I'm supposed to do as his child. He has already given me all the answers I need to get through life. They are written in his Word, the Bible. I simply need to read it daily and do the things it tells me to do. It's really not rocket science. He has already given me all the resources I need. Second Peter 1:3 says, "His divine power has given us everything we need for a godly life through our knowledge of him who called us by his own glory and goodness" (New International Version).

I already have the patience, courage, strength, enthusiasm, self-control, knowledge, perseverance, godliness, and many other resources I need to be successful and live the life God has set apart and designed specifically for me to live. I don't need to pray to God for these things. He has already given them to me through his divine power. I simply need to tap into that divine power and use it. By reading his Word I learn these things, and I can apply them to my life.

As I sat on the floor that day in tears that turned to laughter, I didn't immediately feel strengthened. But that situation gave me hope that God would pull me through this difficult depression. I knew that by reading his Word and staying true to his plan for my life, he would pull me through and set my feet on higher ground. And that's exactly what he did. He has done that through countless other experiences in my life. God's promise is that his Word contains all of the answers we need. If we choose to read it, he will direct our path in life.

If you are not a Christian and don't have a personal relationship with Jesus Christ, you need to make a decision to put your life in his hands and trust him to guide your path. I am not a biblical scholar and do not have the entire Bible memorized. And as you can see, my life is far from perfect. I mess up on a daily (and oftentimes hourly) basis. But truly, the only way I get through each day is to rely on God to lead me. He is where my help comes from. He gives me the strength, encouragement, energy, and motivation I need to continue on to love my kids the way he loves me.

Put your trust in God, and you will still have daily trials and struggles, just like everyone else. But your perspective of those trials and struggles will completely change as God showers you with his grace in difficult times and strength in times of struggle. He loves you with a love that is never-ending. His love will never fail you. I can tell you that from my personal experience. The people of this earth will let you down—your spouse, kids, friends, and family— but God never will.

All you have to do to have a personal relationship with Jesus Christ is simply pray this prayer: "God, I can't do this on my own. I have sinned, and I continue to mess up daily. Please forgive me of my sins and cleanse my life. I need you to help me and guide my life. Please come into my heart, take over my life, and lead me in the direction you want my life to go. I give it all to you. In Jesus' name, I pray. Amen." It's that simple. Admit that you can't do it on your own and you need God to direct your path. The moment you do that, your life will forever be changed. The Holy Spirit will help you daily, and your life will have a new purpose and meaning. You will be completely forgiven and become a new creation in Jesus.

Second Corinthians 5:17 says, "Therefore, if anyone is in Christ, the new creation has come: the old has gone, the new is here!" (NIV). You will be able to start new from this day forward and lead the life you were meant to lead. It will truly be the best decision you ever make. You will not only have God to lead you here on earth, but also eternity in heaven. What do you have to lose? If you're anything like me, and you've tried it on your own, and it's not working, then turn toward Jesus. He is the only answer and the only one who can change your life.

Chapter 2

Plans Aren't Everything

Set your minds on things above, not on earthly things.
—Colossians 3:2 (NIV)

If someone had warned me that becoming an adult was so difficult, I would have stayed a child forever. Adults are responsible for paying bills, holding down a job, doing housework and yard work, cooking, grocery shopping—the list goes on forever. When you become a parent, the amount of responsibilities you have doubles or even triples.

I am one of those people who likes to have everything in order. I am not a perfectionist, but I like to be organized and neat. I make a menu for the week based around any commitments and then grocery shop accordingly. I prepare for upcoming birthday parties, dinners, etc., oftentimes weeks in advance. I like to have my house clean. I have even been known to plan activities for an entire upcoming summer several months in advance, just to make sure I have plenty of activities to keep my kids entertained each day. I am a planner. I come by this very naturally, as my mom is "Martha Stewart on steroids"!

When my older boys were two and four, we took a family trip to Disney World. My parents and sister were with us, so all the details of the trip were planned out. Tickets were purchased, and we arrived at our time share ready for fun. The first two days of the trip sailed by smoothly. We all had a blast. We went to Disney World the first day and then followed it up with the Animal Kingdom the second day. We had a five-day pass to all of the Disney theme parks, so we still had three fun-filled days ahead of us—or so we thought!

The third day greeted us with two-year-old Eli vomiting in his crib at 2:00 a.m., then again at 3:00 a.m., and again at 4:00 a.m. I had one spare set of sheets, but after the third round of vomiting, that poor child was sleeping on hotel towels in his crib. It was not a pretty scene for anyone involved. By 8:00 a.m., the vomiting seemed to have stopped. My sister, who is a pediatric nurse practitioner, checked him out. (I highly recommend bringing one of those along with you on vacation!) Since he had no fever or any other symptoms consistent with a virus or other illness, she concluded that it must have been something he ate. None of the rest of our family was sick, so we felt sure he was not contagious. It had been about three hours since he last vomited.

We had a decision to make. We flew all the way to Florida. This may be the only time my children would get to experience Disney World. The entire family was there together enjoying our vacation. Do we stay in the hotel room with a possibly sick baby who seemed to be much better and miss a day, maybe two or three, at the parks, or do we go to Disney World anyway? We had to consider my four-year-old son as well as the rest of the family who was there with us. We decided to brave the park.

Our family arrived at the park around 10:00 a.m. with smiling faces ready to have a wonderful family day together. Being the huge planner that I am, and by the urging of my mom, I had packed tons of supplies just in case Eli got sick again. But we were fairly confident that would not happen. I mean, we were at Disney World. It's the "happiest place on earth," right? What could happen? Nonetheless, we had a couple of changes of clothes for him, water to keep him hydrated, medicine, baby wipes, etc. I was feeling pretty good about our day at that point.

The carousel was the first ride we had planned. It was now around 10:15 a.m. We stepped into the long line, awaiting our turn. We had been in line for approximately three seconds when Eli suddenly vomits without warning. He was laughing and giggling one minute, and then it just came out. And came out. And came out. I apologize for the disgusting visual image, but it's important to the chapter or I would have left it out.

Since I was so prepared, you'd think this was no big deal. I mean, I was a Girl Scout for years. Our motto was "Always be prepared," or something like that. Maybe that's the Boy Scout motto; who knows? Anyway, I was prepared. Go me! However, what I didn't plan on was the fact that I'd be holding Eli at the moment he decided to vomit. He completely nailed me! I had vomit on my face, in my mouth (since I was talking to him at that moment—lucky me), in my hair, down my shirt, inside my shirt clinging to my bra, on my pants, soaking through my tennis shoes, and in every place on my body you can possibly imagine. No, I'm not exaggerating! All I could think was, *I didn't bring any clothes for me! How could I not bring clothes for me?*

So I now had another choice to make. As I stood there in the middle of a crowd of very sympathetic people at Disney World (did I mention this is the "happiest place on earth"?) covered in vomit, and smelling quite lovely, I might add, should I ruin everyone's day and go back to the hotel to shower and change? Or do I go buy a new shirt, wipe myself off with baby wipes, and push through?

I'm proud to say I'm now the owner of a new Mickey Mouse shirt! It took a good, solid hour to clean the vomit out of my mouth and off my face, hair, bra, tennis shoes, and every other place you could possibly imagine. On a positive note, I looked so disgusting and miserable that all of the sweet ladies in the thirty-minute-long line in the bathroom allowed me to cut in line. There is a silver lining! I could smell myself all day long, as could the rest of my family. But that day at Disney World was truly magical. My boys had the best time! Watching their laughter and joy as they rode the rides, met Mickey Mouse, ate junk food, and played to their little hearts' content made the vomit smell worth it. I wouldn't go back and change it for the world. Okay, maybe I would go back and have my husband holding Eli if I could change it. Just kidding; apparently, that's not nice! I'm also happy to report that there was no more vomit for the remainder of the trip, and there was no argument about who got the first shower when we arrived back at our time share that evening!

My point in telling you that truly disgusting story is that kids are going to cause your plans to change countless times throughout your life. They might get sick, as my little Eli did. They might have some sort of accident. They might make a mess. They might need an "attitude adjustment," as my mom always called it. There will always be something that will cause your plans to change, need to be adjusted, and sometimes canceled. But it's all in how you react and your attitude that sets the tone for your kids.

If you teach your children that everything is ruined and you give up on your plans when something goes wrong, that is how they will respond to negative situations in life. But if you teach your children to go with the flow, adjust, and find the positive in negative situations, then that is how they will respond. What type of adults do you want your children to become? I know I want mine to become adults who are easy to work with and can adapt in any kind of situation. Teach them how to become adaptable by modeling it yourself in your everyday life. You will be giving them a gift that is infinitely important for the rest of their lives.

Chapter 3

Set and Stick to Your Priorities

*Wherever your treasure is, there the desires of your
heart will also be.*—Luke 12:34 (NLT)

God. Family. Friends. Everything else. Those are the priorities our family has set. We very intentionally sat down and put those priorities in place several years ago, using the Bible as our guide. There have been times in our marriage where we have not always honored our priorities in that order, and we have noticed that it throws our family out of balance when we don't keep them in order.

After the birth of our second son, my husband and I were both working full-time. I was a teacher and he was working for a large commercial construction company. If you're not familiar with the construction industry, many of the jobs are completed during the evenings, weekends, and the wee hours of the morning. If roads need to be closed down to complete a project, it cannot be done during peak traffic hours, so they close the roads down and work at night. In addition, like many other fields, money is the top priority. There are always strict deadlines for when work needs to be completed, because everything builds on each other to get a job completed. It's actually pretty amazing to see how everything comes together to build these huge buildings. Inevitably, weather conditions such as rain, heavy winds, etc., causes delays in the schedules, and these construction companies and subcontractors are always running behind.

All that being said, my husband left for work sometime during the five o'clock hour each morning and didn't return home generally until around 7:30 or 8:00 p.m. He worked several weekends each month in addition to those long hours during the week. My boys woke up each morning after he had already left for work and they went to bed before he had returned home each evening. This meant the boys did not see their dad during the week at all, and they frequently didn't see him during the weekend either. I felt like a single mom. I'm sure many of you are in similar situations, or you might actually be a single mom or dad. If so, I truly feel for you, as I know those years were some of the most difficult. I was constantly exhausted from getting the boys ready and to school each morning, working all day, then picking them up from school, cooking dinner, bathing them, and getting them to bed each day by myself.

After many, many discussions with my husband, we realized our priorities were out of whack. He was often missing church when he had to work on Sundays, which wasn't putting God first. He was missing out on some of the most valuable time in our children's lives, so he wasn't putting our family second in our priority list. And he had no time for friends with that crazy schedule. Our marriage was suffering. Our family was suffering, and we just never felt like we could get ahead financially. But he felt trapped in his job. He had an incredible retirement package and the best benefits package you could possibly get. We didn't pay a dime for health insurance, and we had the highest coverage there was. His salary was excellent. The tradeoff was that he had to be available whenever his company needed him, regardless of any other commitments or priorities he might have.

We knew this was not the life God wanted for us or our family. So after years and years of prayer, we felt God was leading my husband to quit his job and move to a more family-oriented company. Through a series of events, he was offered a great job at a wonderful company, but the pay and benefits were significantly less. With the economy the way it was, this was going to be a crazy leap of faith to take a pay cut, not to mention he would now be starting over at a new company. You never want to be low man on the totem pole at a company in a bad economy, because if the company needs to make cuts, you are usually the first to go. Additionally, we were now very nervous about our new health coverage, which was nowhere near as good as what we had previously.

But we knew God was leading us in that direction. And we know God is always faithful in taking care of his children when we are obedient. The Bible says, "As the body without the spirit is dead, *so faith without deeds is dead*" (James 2:26 NIV, emphasis added). If we wanted a different life, we had to obey God. When we take the step of obedience, he always shows us his faithfulness and takes care of us. We know that his Word, the Bible, tells us to align our priorities with God's priorities. So we decided to take the leap! It was incredibly scary, to say the least. But we knew what we were currently doing wasn't working for our family. If you want different results, you have to do something different. So we embarked on this new journey.

I can't even begin to count the blessings God has poured out over our family since making that decision. When my husband quit his job, his former company gave him a large sum of money that was part of his profit sharing, and we were able to use that money toward purchasing our dream home, something we could never have afforded if he hadn't quit his job. Following that, God blessed us with our third son. We would never have been able to afford, nor would I have ever considered having another child because I was already struggling taking care of the two boys by myself. My husband's new job allowed him to work an eight-to-five schedule Monday through

Friday and no weekends, while offering him an additional week of paid vacation each year. He now had the opportunity to attend all of our boys' sporting events, school programs, etc. Additionally, he's home for dinner every single evening, and we get to enjoy dinner as a family. Also, with our extra time, we were able to step up and become the leaders of our Bible study group, where we grew so much in our faith during those two years of leadership.

And here's the biggest blessing of all (well, right there with the blessing of little Logan). My husband took a pay cut, we bought a nicer, larger home, we had another son, and then we still had enough money for me to quit my job and stay home with my boys within two years of this decision. Only in God's economy (as our pastor likes to say) does that add up. The Bible says, "Whoever can be trusted with very little can also be trusted with much, and whoever is dishonest with very little will also be dishonest with much. So if you have not been trustworthy in handling worldly wealth, who will trust you with true riches?" (Luke 16:10–11 NIV). This Bible verse is generally used in connection with discussions of tithing. However, I often recall this verse in my life in regard to obedience. When I am obedient with the little things God asks me to do, he can trust me to be obedient in the bigger things. When I am obedient in the little things as well as the big things, God can trust me with "true riches." I believe that because my husband and I had been obedient over the years to God's Word, and then when he asked us to be obedient in this huge decision, he poured out the "true riches" over our family.

In our lives, we have found that when we align our priorities with God's priorities, and we are obedient to his calling, he will bless us beyond anything we can ever imagine. Ephesians 3:20 says, "Now to him who is able to do immeasurably more than all we ask or imagine, according to his power that is at work within us" (NIV). I can't even put a price tag on the time I get to spend with my husband and my children every single day now that my husband is working at his new job. And I know if we keep our priorities in line, we will leave a legacy for our children and grandchildren and many generations beyond them. It's all about teaching our children that God should always be first and we should always follow his will, family should always be second, followed by friends, and everything else can fit in behind those things. God is able and willing to bless your family beyond your wildest imagination. Trust him, obey him, and watch what he'll do in your life.

Chapter 4

You Can't Screw Them Up Too Badly

"My grace is enough; it's all you need. My strength comes into its own in your weakness." Once I heard that, I was glad to let it happen. I quit focusing on the handicap and began appreciating the gift. It was a case of Christ's strength moving in on my weakness. Now I take limitations in stride, and with good cheer, these limitations that cut me down to size—abuse, accidents, opposition, bad breaks. I just let Christ take over! And so the weaker I get, the stronger I become.—2 Corinthians 12:9–10 (The Message)

When my two older boys were two and four, they shared a bedroom. After having done that for a couple of years, I wouldn't recommend it if you can avoid it! At one point during this period, they caught a little cold. My husband, Matt, and I were just heading to bed for the night when we heard coughing coming from the boys' bedroom. I asked Matt, "Which one is that?" as it was very difficult to distinguish between our kids on a baby monitor. He said it was Luke, our oldest. So I sneaked into the bedroom and gave Luke some cough medicine. Then we went to bed, and tried to sleep. The coughing continued on and off, but we couldn't administer more cough medicine for another four hours. We lay awake in bed waiting and listening. We went into the boys' bedroom twice more during the night to administer more cough medicine to Luke. At this point, we were exhausted having been up most of the night. And I, like most people, am super pleasant when I get almost no sleep. You can imagine what my attitude was like. (Can you sense the sarcasm?)

Around 4:00 a.m. Luke called us to take him to the bathroom. I begrudgingly dragged myself out of bed and took him. While he was going potty, he looked at me, and rubbing his sleepy little eyes, said, "Mommy, can you please give Eli some cough medicine? He's been keeping me up all night!"

The wheels began to turn in my mind as I realized what had happened. I'd been giving the wrong kid cough medicine all night! Had I realized this fact hours ago, then maybe we would have gotten some sleep. My anger began to build, and unfortunately, I lost my temper. Something I often do when I've had no sleep.

I proceeded to yell at my husband, "Matt, get in here! I've been giving the wrong kid cough medicine all night and it's all your fault!" It's amazing that man still loves me after my outbursts. He looked at me bewildered, as he'd just been awakened from his dream-filled sleep. He stood there trying to understand what I was saying through blinking eyes. Then you could see the lightbulb moment. He understood. Ugh!

He gave Eli some cough medicine, and we tucked Luke back into bed. And go figure, we were able to sleep for another hour before our alarms sounded at 5:00 a.m. Another sleepless night, the life of a parent. But this one was our own fault, which made it that much more frustrating.

We learned two lessons that night. The first is that having children share a room is a bad idea. The second is that you can't screw your children up too badly. My sister, who is the best pediatric nurse practitioner there is, always says, "Kids are pretty resilient."

And she's right; children are very resilient. There are obviously things you should never do to your children, such as abuse, neglect, etc. But basically, all parents are going to mess up from time to time. In my case, on a daily basis! But what you need to remember is that tomorrow is new day. You are not a terrible mother or father just because you messed up. Don't beat yourself up over what you have done wrong. Simply make the choice to be a better parent tomorrow and correct the mistakes you have made. God extends his perfect grace to you when you mess up. Accept his grace. God's grace will never end. Give yourself a break. Forgive yourself for your mistakes, as God has already forgiven you for them, and move on to tomorrow.

When you vow to fix your mistakes and not repeat them, you become a better parent. You might mess something else up or make a different mistake tomorrow. But you will learn from that one as well and not repeat it. It's a process, and you have to take it a day at a time. You won't be able to perfect it, but you can work on it one "screw up" at a time. Each day, you will become a better parent.

Learn from your own mistakes, as well as the mistakes of others. For instance, always check before administering cough medicine to a child to make sure you know who is actually coughing. See? There's a mistake you never have to make! Learn, learn, learn. Never stop learning and trying, and give yourself the grace to mess up. You are not perfect, nor will you ever be. Regardless of the show others put on, they are not perfect either. Strive to be the best parent you can be. God placed your children in your care because he knew you were exactly what that child needed. God knows your heart, and he knows you love your children. He expects you to make mistakes. He even welcomes those mistakes, so he can extend forgiveness and grace to you. As long as your heart is in the right place, God will use each situation, mistake, or otherwise for your good. Romans 8:28 says, "And we know that in all things God works for the good of those who love Him, who have been called according to His purpose" (NIV).

He loves you and wants the best for your life and for the lives of your children. He has a perfect purpose for your life. Extend yourself the grace that God extends to you daily. Don't worry so much about messing up but focus on what you can do better tomorrow. Rest in the hope that God will use your mistakes for his good and the good of your children.

Chapter 5

Spend Individual Time with Each of Your Kids

Children are a gift from the Lord; they are a reward from him.
—Psalm 127:3 (NLT)

As adults, most of us crave attention. We don't necessarily want to be in the spotlight, but we want our loved ones to pay attention to us. We want them to listen when we are speaking, pay attention to our needs and wants, and spend quality time with us. Our children have those same desires. They desperately want the listening ear of their parents, their parents' approval, and the attention that we all crave.

My boys absolutely love swimming. For some strange yet wonderful reason, the swimming pool seems to be the only place we go where my boys don't fight. I can't explain it, but I'm so thankful. So you can imagine, we go swimming *a lot*! Being a stay-at-home mom, we don't have a lot of money lying around. Our neighborhood pool is free. So it's a win-win for everyone involved.

Every single time we go swimming, the same thing happens. The second my two older boys get into the water, they start yelling, "Mommy, watch me!" No exaggeration, they will each utter this phrase fifty to one hundred times in a two-hour period while we're at the pool. Even Logan, our youngest, has started mimicking this phrase, "Mommy, wa' me!" It doesn't matter what they are doing— flips under the water, jumps off the side of the pool, swimming from one end of the pool to the other—they want my complete, undivided attention. The only problem is, there is only one of me and three of them. There is no way to give them that complete, undivided attention. While it is rather annoying after hearing the same thing hundreds of times, it is also sweet in its own way. I love that they care so much about my approval and they crave my praise and attention.

Group outings with the entire family are wonderful and incredibly important. Children need to see that they are members of a family unit. They need to see that each member of the family is equally loved, but no one in the family holds more value than the others. We need to teach our children to share time as well as possessions. It is so important for our kids to understand that they cannot have our sole, undivided attention all the time. If we teach them that, they will grow into healthy, well-rounded adults. I often say to my kids, "The world does not revolve around you, nor does our family. We are a family, so we share and help each other. It's not just about you." I truly want them to understand this principal, because I don't want them to grow into adults who feel like everything is about them and everyone else should focus on them and do things for them. I want my kids to be others'-centered. I want them to care about others and always think of what they can do for others or how they can help those around them. They will not think like that if the focus is always on them.

That being said, it is so important to set apart time on a regular basis to spend with each of your children individually. You may set out time each day, once a week, or once a month. However you choose to do it, it needs to be intentional and regular.

When you set that time apart for each child, do something that is special to him or her and that fits his or her interests. Eli, my middle child, loves pancakes more than anything else in the world. Even more than he loves Santa! So when we have our special time together, we generally go eat pancakes at IHOP. That's all he needs to be the happiest boy in the world.

In contrast, my oldest son couldn't care less about food. He's all about his Legos. So when he and I get our individual time together, we generally go browse the Lego store at the mall and pick out a small new Lego set for him. That makes him feel really special. Study your children, discover their interests, and show them that you care by sharing in what is special to them.

I do have to admit since having our third child, this individual time is something I struggle with making a priority. I was a working mom until about six months ago, and my two older boys are actively involved in sports, we were leading our Bible study group at church for the past two years, we serve each week at the visitors' booth at our church, etc. We lead a very busy life, as the majority of people do. This is something very difficult to fit into our busy schedule. That being said, I urge you to make this a priority. I have seen such a difference in the behavior, actions, and attitudes of my boys when I make individual time with them a priority. It does wonders for their self-esteem and makes such a difference in the type of relationship I share with each of them.

Start small if you feel you don't have the time, or if you have multiple children and aren't sure how to make time for each. Here are some suggestions you can try that I have found successful over the years. Put the other kids to bed at the normal bedtime, and stay up reading an extra bedtime story with one of your kids who loves reading. Turn on a cartoon for your other children, and spend time playing a board game with your child who loves games. Go into the backyard and spend time playing catch with one of your kids, while the others jump on the trampoline or ride bikes. Utilize any family members who live near you. Ask if your other kids can visit their house for an afternoon or evening, or even if they can spend the night and have a fun slumber party with one of your children. Send your other children to the playroom, and have one of your children who loves to cook help you make dinner or bake cookies. If you have a little one, as I do, take advantage of nap time. Spend time building a Lego car or playing dolls with your older child, while the younger is napping. If the oldest still naps, allow him to skip his nap one day and make it a special event to get to spend that time with you. These are just a few ideas, but there are so many more. Be creative! Be intentional! And make this a priority!

Writing this chapter has even motivated me to do a better job at this. I have seen the benefits of this concept over the years, and I know the importance of it. It will make such a tremendous difference in the lives of your children. Invest in them, and you will reap great benefits. Galatians 6:7 says, "A man reaps what he sows" (NIV). What are you sowing in your children?

Chapter 6

Find the Positive in Every Situation

Always be joyful. Never stop praying. Be thankful in all circumstances, for this is God's will for you who belong to Christ Jesus.—1 Thessalonians 5:16–18 (NLT)

It was Christmas Day, and we were with my parents, my sister and brother-in-law, my nephew, my husband, and our kids in a cabin in Broken Bow, Oklahoma. It was an amazing trip, with wonderful family time. We had been there for four days leading up to Christmas, and it was our final day. On that day, God blessed us with a beautiful snow, a white Christmas. Living in Texas for almost ten years, you can imagine how beautiful that was to see since it rarely even gets cold enough to snow. What an amazing blessing!

Our boys played in the snow all day and had an absolutely wonderful time! Then everything began to change. Just as the sun started to set for the evening, we lost power in our cabin. We were in the middle of the woods, it was getting dark, and we were in a state we knew was not well-equipped to handle snow, as it rarely snows in southern Oklahoma. So we knew this was going to be a long night, and the electric company probably would not be able to get the power turned back on for quite some time. The heater in the cabin was electric, so it went out with the power, as well as the electric stove we were using to cook our dinner. At that moment, I had never been more in love with my Eagle Scout husband, who had packed extra flashlights and tons of emergency supplies. However, we still did not have a way to combat the eminent issue of keeping the family warm through the night.

I immediately began to worry, as I would assume most moms would. I had a one-year-old, four-year-old, and five-and-a-half-year-old, and I had to find a way to keep them warm in a snowstorm with no electricity. Praise God that we had a gas fireplace! I bundled the boys in two pairs of pajamas, and we cuddled up next to the fireplace with nice, warm blankets. That worked well for a while, but it was getting increasingly colder in the cabin as it grew darker outside, and the heat inside the cabin began to dissipate.

At that moment, in the midst of my worry, sitting there by the candlelight, my four-year-old son, Eli, brought tears to my eyes and a smile filled with joy to my face. He said to everyone, "At least we have each odder [other]!" Wow! Talk about melting a momma's heart. That child at such a young age understood what was important in life.

Eli reminded us all about how to find joy in all situations, even when you are worried, scared, or uncertain. Regardless of your circumstances, regardless of the fear surrounding you, regardless of your worry, look for joy. His words changed the atmosphere of that room. Rather than focus on the negative situation at hand, we can focus on the positive. We can shift our focus to the good things God has given us. Family. Shelter. Food (even if it was cold!). Christmas stories to read. Blankets. Extra pajamas. Candles to light the room. Flashlights. Beds to sleep in. I can go on and on. We were so very blessed, even in the midst of a difficult situation. The Bible says in Philippians 4:8, "Finally, brothers and sisters, whatever is true, whatever is noble, whatever is right, whatever is pure, whatever is lovely, whatever is admirable—if anything is excellent or praiseworthy—think about such things" (NIV). Redirect your focus, and it will change your perspective.

I try to remember those words daily as I am faced with trials or struggles of any kind. When my two oldest sons were tested and found to have some severe food allergies, I'm sad to say my first thoughts were very negative. I felt overwhelmed about how I was going to find foods to cook that they could eat, how I was going to handle this situation with day care, and what I would do about taking my kids to restaurants. There were tears shed, and lots of anger and frustration. Then I remembered Philippians 4:8, and I chose to change my focus to those things that were true, noble, right, pure, lovely, admirable, excellent, and praiseworthy. I reminded myself that my boys were healthy. I remembered that they were full of energy and life. I remembered that I was blessed to have these beautiful boys, and that we could adapt to whatever situation was thrown at us because we were already equipped with God's strength to handle it.

When my husband and I are struggling in our marriage, I remember that I am thankful to have a husband who loves me and is an amazing father to my boys. When I am struggling with fighting and disobedient children, I remember that I am thankful to have my children. Sometimes it is difficult to find the joy, but it is always there if you look hard enough. My mom often says to me, "Someday you'll look back on these situations and laugh." I generally respond by saying, "I'm not so sure." But I know she is right, as she is one of the wisest people I know. Find joy in some part of every situation, and you will truly live a happier, more blessed life.

Chapter 7

Creative Discipline

Point your kids in the right direction—when they're
old they won't be lost.—Proverbs 22:6 (MSG)

I honestly don't even know where to begin with this chapter. Throughout the years, my husband and I have tried it all when it comes to discipline. We've tried positive reinforcement such as sticker charts, treat jars, offering candy, and earning rewards. We've tried punishments such as timeouts, spankings, removal of toys, removal of privileges, a consequence jar, and many, many more!

I've learned that discipline is one of the most difficult parts of parenting but also one of the most important. If you don't discipline your children, you are setting them up for failure in the future. Discipline has always had a very negative connotation to me, but it truly is not. I now think of discipline as using resources and tools to train and mold your children into making good decisions in the future when you are not there to guide them. Discipline is a positive part of parenting because discipline is how we teach our children. Without it, there would be no opportunity for learning or growth.

My husband once said to me, "Jennifer, they are children. You can't expect them to behave all the time." I know that probably seems obvious to most of you, but it was eye-opening to me. I expected my children to be well behaved. I expected them to always tell the truth. I expected them to share their toys. I expected them to do what I asked when I asked them to do it. I expected them to make safe choices. I expected them to be nice to each other and not fight. I mean, these are all rules in our home. Why wouldn't my children follow them? They know the rules. They know there will be consequences if they don't follow the rules. Why aren't they listening? I was beyond frustrated with reminding them of the same rules over and over again, and them breaking the same rules over and over again. So when my husband said those words to me, it really stuck in my head. Of course they are going to break the rules and not do the right thing quite frequently. They are kids. They have not yet completely developed the ability to reason. They have not yet acquired the proper problem-solving skills. You can't expect them to reason and behave like an adult would.

So what does that mean in terms of discipline? Yes, you can absolutely expect your children to misbehave. What should you do when they misbehave? Now here's the really frustrating part. It depends on the situation, on the behavior, on the age, on the number of times they've committed the infraction, on the type of child you have, etc. There are so many factors, which I suppose is why we didn't receive a manual on how to parent when our children were born. That sure would have been helpful! I'm just going to tell you some things I've tried that have worked and some that haven't. I'm still learning this myself, so feel free to e-mail me with any ideas you have as well! I'm willing to try almost anything!

Discipline Changes as Your Child Changes

The first thing I've learned through trial and error is that the punishment or positive reinforcement that worked really well last week or last month may not continue to work this week. My oldest son, Luke, is a child who hates to be alone. When he first started being able to toddle about the house, instead of playing in the living room in the area where I set the toys out for him, he would actually pick up his toys and bring them to the kitchen where I was. It didn't matter that I was only ten feet away from him, and he could see me from where his toys were. He would place the toys at my feet and sit there to play while I cooked or washed dishes or whatever I might be doing. He couldn't stand to be in the other room away from me. That's actually pretty cute now that I think back on it.

As Luke got older and we acquired a few more toys thanks to grandparents who spoil our children rotten, we decided to turn one of the rooms into a playroom. We thought this was a brilliant plan! The toys would be out of sight, there would be less clutter, and Luke would have a fun place to play. What we had forgotten was Luke's need to be near us at all times. So rather than playing in his playroom, he would go get the toys he wanted and again bring them to play right at my feet. You get the picture. So what we figured out fairly quickly was that timeout was a great punishment for Luke when he did something wrong. Since he couldn't stand to be away from us, separating him by putting him in another room for a set amount of time was a great way to deter bad behavior. At least this worked for a while.

Now like I stated above, what worked last week might not work this week. As Luke got older, he wasn't as concerned about being with us at all times. Separating him by putting him in timeout was no longer effective. He would simply shrug off the timeout, go to his room, serve it, and come back unaffected. Once we discovered that wasn't working, we had to come up with a new idea.

At this older age, we discovered Luke was really motivated by toys, so that's when we started a sticker chart. The chart had several rows. When Luke did something really good, such as following directions and completing a chore, doing something helpful without being asked, using his manners, behaving appropriately at school, etc., he would get to put a sticker on his chart. Once he filled up a row, he got to choose a toy from the "treasure chest." Now, before you start thinking this is crazy and would cost a lot of money, let me tell you where these "treasure chest" toys came from. For the first four years of my child's life, he had no idea that his "happy meal" or "wacky pack" or whatever the meal might be called at a fast-food restaurant came with a toy. Before the meal ever made it to the table, the toy magically disappeared. He received his kid's meal, and he was a happy camper. I put those toys in a special basket in a closet, and he was none the wiser. I thought I might need them for something one day, and sure enough, this was the day. So now I had plenty of toys to fill up Luke's "treasure chest," and he loved earning them. My point is, don't spend a lot of money. Be creative. Go to the dollar store, or the Dollar Spot at Target. These don't need to be extravagant toys.

However, just like before, the sticker chart worked for a while. Then the excitement and newness of that wore off, and we needed to change our plan again. It's like the old saying goes, "If you always do what you've always done, then you'll always get what you've always gotten." Translation to parenting: "If you keep doing the same thing and it's not working, then try changing it up." Your child has probably outgrown that approach. Mix it up, keep it new, and be creative.

Each Child Has Unique Needs

Another thing I've found about disciplining my children is that the needs of each child are so different. One of Luke's favorite phrases is, "That's not fair!" I often smart off with, "Don't get me started about what's not fair!" However, a better response might be, "Fair does not always mean equal treatment." The discipline strategy that works well for one child may not be effective at all for your other children. For example, Eli, our middle son, couldn't care less about toys. If they're there, he'll play with them. But if not, he'll find some other way to entertain himself. Luke, on the other hand, is greatly motivated by toys.

We were having some major issues with our boys not being thankful for what they had been given. Imagine that! Children in America not being thankful! Hard to believe, right? Our boys were not taking care of the toys they had. They were refusing to clean up their playroom. They were asking for new toys. They were complaining about their toys not being good enough. My husband and I finally had enough. Our boys are beyond blessed! They have more toys than Toys "R" Us thanks to their very loving and generous grandparents. We decided to put our foot down and tackle this problem once and for all. We refused to raise spoiled brats who don't appreciate what they have. So we decided the only way to teach the boys to be thankful for what they had was to take everything away and make them earn it back. After all, when you are forced to work hard for something, you appreciate it so much more, right? This strategy seemed flawless to us!

We took all of the toys out of the boys' rooms (and we even made them help), put everything into the playroom, and locked the playroom doors. The boys had no access to toys. We reiterated our household rules, discussed the ungrateful behaviors that led to this, and explained to the boys how they could begin earning their toys back.

By the end of the first day, Luke had already earned five toys back. He was behaving perfectly, and we were so excited that it was working! However, Eli had only earned one toy back by the end of the first day. We were bewildered. Why would a child not want to earn his toys back? Shouldn't he be doing everything we discussed? We just didn't understand it, until we really thought about it: Eli is not at all motivated by toys. If he has no toys available to him, he's perfectly fine and will find another way to entertain himself. So losing all his toys was no big deal. He was not going to change his behavior. Therefore, we concluded, we needed to find something different to motivate him. So we continued allowing Luke to earn his toys back, and we strategized about what to do with Eli.

After giving it plenty of thought, we found the only thing Eli cared about losing was his blanket. Eli loves his blanket. He sleeps with it at bedtime and naptime and often tries to sneak it out of his bed throughout the day when I'm not paying attention. Losing his blanket at bedtime would be the end of the world for him. We were fairly confident that the threat of losing that blanket would deter him from misbehaving, and we were right (for a while, until we had to change it up again!).

Of course it's difficult as parents to explain to your children why they are not receiving the same consequences. Children don't always completely understand the concept, especially younger children, but it's a concept they'll understand as they get older. I believe it's an important concept to grasp for later in life as well. You won't always be treated exactly the same because we're all different and we all have different needs. I think this is a very effective way to teach your children from a young age that life may not always be equal. It is much more important to be treated as an individual and have your individual needs met. God created every single person different because we all have a unique purpose. We need to always remember that in the way we interact with our children. Foster each of your children's unique personalities in a way that meets their individual needs and helps them achieve their purpose in life.

Stay Consistent

A third thing I've learned the hard way, like most things in my life, is to stay consistent in discipline. My children are creatures of habit and schedule. I am a very schedule-oriented person. I like to have my day planned out, and I like to keep a schedule so everyone knows what to expect and when to expect it. I've found that it reduces questions, whining, and complaining and keeps order in our home. I've noticed that whenever we deviate from our schedule even slightly, utter chaos ensues in our home!

My parents came to town from Oklahoma to visit one weekend. They do this quite frequently. They arrived on Friday afternoon, and as usual, my sister and her husband and their children came over for a big family dinner. We were all outside playing in the backyard and grilling. Everyone was having a great time.

Suddenly it occurred to Luke that he didn't know what we were eating for dinner. He always has to know what's for breakfast, lunch, dinner, and snacks each day. He loves food (just like his mom) so he stops playing to come find out what we're eating and what time dinner will be ready. I told him what we were having, and he followed up with, "What's for dessert?"

I responded, "We're not having dessert." Oh my! I thought the world was going to end right then and there when he heard that news.

He immediately started whining and complaining, "But, we always have dessert when Mimi and Papa [my mom and dad] come to town. That's not fair" (his favorite and my least favorite phrase of all time).

In his defense, that is a true statement. We almost always have dessert when Mimi and Papa come over, and most of the time when any company comes over. He was in such a habit of having dessert when company came over that he just didn't know what to do with himself when he couldn't have it.

In addition to the dessert fiasco, we let our two older boys stay up an hour past their bedtime that same night. I figured it was no big deal. We had company. It's a rare occasion to let them stay up late. What was it going to hurt? (Those are famous last words.)

See, my boys don't understand the concept of sleeping in. It doesn't matter if they go to bed at their normal bedtime or five hours past bedtime, they still wake up sometime during the six o'clock hour every single day. I seriously don't understand what the matter is with these children! If they only knew how wonderful sleep was! Nonetheless, they wake up bright-eyed and ready to go very early each morning. If you haven't guessed, I'm not a morning person!

So bright and early the next morning, the boys popped up and were ready to go. But I quickly realized the hour less sleep they got the night before was having quite an effect on them. The fighting began almost immediately, as did the whining, complaining, yelling, and hurting each other. I could tell this was going to be a long day.

I'm telling you this story to illustrate two points. Children are creatures of habit. If you do something out of the norm, it generally has an effect on them in some way. Not having dessert as they expected caused whining and complaining. Staying up late and not getting enough sleep caused a long day of bad attitudes. Kids need consistency in order to behave the way you'd like them to behave.

So what does this have to do with discipline? You must also be consistent in your discipline. When you give kids a rule to follow, you need to be consistent in having them follow it. If the rule is "No wrestling in the living room" (you can tell I have boys, right?), then there needs to be a consequence when they start to wrestle in the living room. If you allow it, even just one time, then kids will take advantage of the situation. I know it seems crazy. Those sweet little innocent children would never take advantage of you as parents, right? (Can you sense the sarcasm in my voice?) If you allow them to wrestle in the living room one time, the next time they try to do it and you tell them to stop, you'll immediately be met with arguing and complaining. They'll see that there are cracks in the armor. "Mom allows me to wrestle in the living room when she is too tired to fight with me about it." Or, "Mom allows me to wrestle in the living room when she's on the phone and isn't paying much attention to me."

What happens next is they'll try to break other rules while you're too tired to deal with them or while you're on the phone— or fill in the blank with the situation that occurs at your house. So they'll begin to jump on the furniture or color on the walls or whatever else children do to misbehave. In short, they'll push the limits to see what they can get away with. If you are consistent at all times, regardless of the situation, your children are much less likely to break the established rules of the house or resist you when you discipline them for breaking those rules. There will be nothing for them to argue with you about. You simply say, "You know the rules of the house and you chose to break them. You know the consequence for breaking that rule, so accept your consequence."

It seems so simple, but staying consistent has been such a struggle for me. However, I've seen firsthand how important and effective it is, so I've made it my goal to strive for consistency every day with my children, and it has had a huge impact on attitudes and behavior in our home.

Follow Through with What You Say

This one is pretty straightforward. Your word is only as good as your actions. If I promise my boss I'll have a document on his desk by 4:00 p.m. and it's not there on time, my word means nothing. If I tell my friend I'll pray for her but then I forget, my word means nothing. If I tell my husband I'll stop by the store on my way home from work but leave work late and don't have time to stop, my word means nothing. You get the picture. Every now and again it might happen that you break your word. But when it becomes a regular and natural habit, people don't take you seriously when you say you will do something but don't.

The same is true with our children. Each afternoon my older two boys have one chore that they have to complete before they can earn their afternoon playtime. My husband and I decided it was important to teach our children how to do chores so they would be able to do them when they live on their own. Additionally, we think it is important to teach our children to be contributors in our home. They don't pay the bills or buy the groceries, so they essentially have to earn their keep as we tell them. "You live in our home for free, so you help complete the chores."

Some of the chores are really simple, such as putting clean laundry away, or picking up the toys in their bedroom. Others take a little more time and effort. Luke does almost all his chores without ever complaining or fighting with me. I stress the word *almost* because the one chore I can always count on him to whine and complain about and refuse to do is cleaning up the playroom. In his defense, our playroom is ridiculous! We have more toys in it than Toys "R" Us. I'll be the first to tell you it is out of control. My boys have some of the best grandparents and aunts and uncles in the world. They love to spoil our children rotten by giving them lots of toys. And since there are three boys, we get three times the boy toys at each holiday. So when it comes time to clean the playroom, which we do once a week, Luke throws a fit.

Now I've tried explaining to the boys, particularly Luke, that if they would simply put the toys away as soon as they finish playing with them there wouldn't be a giant mess each week. But trying to get them to follow through with that is as easy as trying to herd cats. It simply can't be done. The boys at this age are incapable of thinking ahead. They jump from toy to toy so quickly they don't stop to think about putting the other toy away. When I'm in the playroom with them, I frequently remind them to stop and put the toy they are playing with away before they get a new one out, but unfortunately, I'm not always in the playroom to remind them. So the playroom is a giant disaster each week when it comes time for that chore.

I always give Luke a whole day's notice when it comes time to clean the playroom again. We clean it every Monday, so I start reminding him about it on Sunday morning. That way it has time to sink in, and he can even get a little jump start on the mess if he'd like. He never does, but at least I'm teaching him that skill now.

When Monday rolls around and it comes time to actually clean the playroom, I sit back and brace for the attack. Luke immediately starts spouting things like, "This isn't my mess! Eli made this mess! Why do I have to clean it?" or "This isn't fair [there's that phrase again] that I have to clean this playroom!" All the while, Eli usually jumps right in and starts cleaning.

The whining goes on and on and on and on and on! I'm sure you can picture it! I always start by reasoning with him. I'll tell him things like, "You are so very blessed to have all these toys. Most kids don't have this many toys. You should be so thankful, and you should want to take care of them." That never works, but maybe one day it will sink in. Then I move on to asking him, "Whose toys are they? Who played with them? So who should have to clean them up?" That never works either, but again, in my dream world it might one day. After that, I move on to reminding him that he's earning his playtime. The sooner he gets his chore finished, the sooner he'll be able to go play. At that point, I usually leave the playroom in an attempt to keep my cool (really so I won't start yelling) and hope and pray that he will simply begin cleaning the playroom. That never works either, and I usually have to repeatedly go back in. This chore generally takes all afternoon because Luke soon manages to bring Eli down to his level. Neither are cleaning, and they usually don't earn their afternoon playtime that day.

Finally in an attempt to stop this madness the following week, I told Luke that if he was so unhappy about cleaning up *his* own toys in *his* playroom, then he wasn't going to be allowed to play in the playroom for an entire week. I thought for sure this would motivate him to get the playroom cleaned that day. Boy, was I ever wrong!

He still fought me, argued with me, whined, and complained all afternoon and did not clean the playroom. So I followed through with the consequence I had given him. He wasn't allowed to set foot in that playroom for the entire week. This may not seem like a terrible consequence to some of you, but the playroom is the only place we keep toys in our home. There are no longer toys in the boys' bedrooms or anywhere else, except for a few baby toys in the living room for Logan. So not being allowed in the playroom means an entire week with no toys at all. And when our entire family goes into the playroom to play, as we often do, he has to find something else to do alone.

This was a very difficult week for him to say the least, and it was a difficult week for me as well. I often use the playroom as a place to send the boys while I'm cooking dinner or bathing the other boys, or working on chores of my own, as a place to keep them occupied. Since I couldn't send Luke in there, it meant keeping him occupied in other ways all week. Consequences oftentimes are just as difficult for the parents as they are for the kids. However, it's well worth it if you come up with an effective consequence and follow through when you say you will.

I'm sure you're wondering if it worked. Why, yes, it did! The very next week, he was allowed back in the playroom. And at the end of that week, it came time to clean the playroom again. Again I gave him a day's notice, and then it came time for him to clean. I tensed, waiting for the attack! And yes, it started to come. But I simply asked him, "Did you enjoy getting to play in your playroom this week?" He immediately stopped, turned around, and began cleaning. Success! Score one point for Mommy, zero for Luke!

Most of the time, that's how it works. When you say you are going to do something, you need to follow through regardless of how painful it is for you. When you don't, your kids learn that your word means nothing. Kids are so much more intelligent than we give them credit for. They are constantly learning. Kids know when you are giving them an empty threat, so don't allow your threats to be empty. When you ask them to clean the playroom without arguing with you or they won't be allowed to play in it for a week, and you don't follow through, they'll argue with you about it the following week. When you tell them to eat their vegetables at dinner or they'll have to eat them for breakfast the next morning, you'd better follow through. If you don't feed them the vegetables for breakfast, your kids won't eat the vegetables the next time you tell them to. Following through with whatever you say is absolutely key in successful discipline.

All of that being said, think before you speak. If you give a consequence, it must be something you can live with and actually follow through on. Again, sadly I speak from experience. Oftentimes in the heat of the moment, I will shout out a consequence either out of anger or because I'm certain it will be severe enough that my kids will do what I want them to do, and I won't have to enforce it. Unfortunately, more often than not, I'm forced to give the consequence. I've been known to tell my kids things like, "If you don't eat your dinner, I'm never giving you dessert again," something I know I'll never be able to uphold. Or I might say something like, "If you continue to behave that way, you'll spend the rest of the day in your bedroom," obviously something you can never do to a four-year-old. I've even said things such as, "If you don't get off the playground right now and come to the car with me, I'll never take you to another park again." I know these things sound ridiculous, but I've said them. And of course my children don't take me seriously when I say them because they know I'll never deliver on those promises.

When doling out a consequence for misbehavior, make sure it's something you can live with and actually deliver. If not, your kids will see that you don't always follow through. And because of that, they'll never take you seriously, and their behavior will not improve.

Spell Out Your Expectations in Advance

If you want your kids to follow your rules, it seems obvious that you would explain your expectations in advance. But we as parents don't always do that. Most of the time, we either yell out rules to our kids in the midst of the moment, or we get upset with them after they've done something wrong. We expect that our kids know the rules and expectations, even if we haven't specifically sat down to explain them. Many of the rules in our home seem obvious to me, but to my kids, they may not be so obvious.

I have two stories to illustrate this point. The first involves Luke, yet again. But since I feel bad that many of my stories in this book revolve around him (mostly because he is my firstborn, and I've messed up so much with him), I'm also going to share an Eli story with you.

It was about 7:00 p.m., and we headed upstairs to start our bedtime routine of baths, Bible story, prayers, and bedtime. We sent Luke, who was five at the time, up ahead of us to play in the playroom, not thinking that would be a problem. This is something we do quite often. We were only about five minutes behind him. I mean, how much trouble can a five-year-old get into in five minutes? (Can you hear the sarcasm in my voice yet again?)

As we arrived at the top of the stairs, we heard a loud banging sound coming from our youngest son, Logan's, room. Baffled, we immediately headed in that direction. As we entered the room, our jaws dropped. Luke, who weighed around forty-five pounds, had climbed into Logan's crib and proceeded to jump up and down wildly in it. Just as we entered the room, the bottom of the crib broke under his weight. This was approximately thirty minutes before bedtime, and now I had no crib for Logan to sleep in.

I calmly looked at my son, told him how much I loved him, gave him a hug, and explained to him that what he did was wrong. Oh, wait! That would have been the perfect parent's response in that situation. Instead, I failed miserably as a parent that day as I lost my temper and proceeded to very loudly (another way of saying yelled) explain to him how jumping on a bed is not only unsafe, it is also not very smart.

Right as I'm in the middle of losing my temper, he innocently says to me, "You never told me not to jump on Logan's bed." What? It seemed so obvious! Jumping on a bed is dangerous. You could get seriously hurt, and you could break the bed (obviously). What do you mean I have to tell you not to jump on Logan's bed? Unfortunately, our kids don't always think before they do, as I assume is the case with most kids. And if they've never been told not to do something, there's a pretty good chance they're going to do it.

I had a similar incidence happen with Eli. This one was not dangerous but was seriously annoying and difficult to clean up. Eli had spent almost two entire days tormenting his little brother, Logan. For some reason, he decided it was his personal duty in life to hurt Logan at least twenty times a day. I have no idea what had gotten into him, but it was driving me (and Logan) insane. After a couple of days of this and crazy amounts of frustration, I finally gave up on consequences and just isolated Eli in his room. I figured that was the only way to keep poor Logan safe.

To my astonishment, Eli went to his room without arguing and sat up there without making a sound for about ten minutes. When his time in his room was up, I called him to come downstairs and offered to give him a second chance (really a fortieth chance) to be nice to his brother. He didn't respond or come downstairs. I called again and waited for a response. Still nothing. Now most of us parents know that when there is no sound coming from a room, that almost always means trouble. Unless they are sound asleep, my kids are never quiet. So when they are, I know they are doing something they should not be doing.

I proceeded upstairs to investigate. When I walked into his room, I looked on in horror. There were stickers covering every single surface I could see, and many I could not see as I discovered later. When I say every single surface, I'm not even exaggerating. He had opened up one of his puzzles and placed a sticker on every single puzzle piece. There were stickers covering his dresser, desk, and bed. He had placed the stickers up and down his doorframe, bedroom door, and closet door. There were stickers cascading down his curtains. You get the picture.

I had to stop, count to ten, and take lots of deep breaths before I could even respond rationally. With the sweetest smile in the world, he looked right at me, beaming with pride, and said, "Look, Mommy, I decorated my room!"

Oh, my word! I was looking around thinking, *The paint is going to peel off the walls when I remove these stickers. This is going to tear the puzzle pieces, rip pages out of his books, make a gooey mess on his furniture, and on and on and on. This is not good.* Apparently I'd never explained to Eli the proper use for stickers. So that day we had a talk about where stickers are allowed to go and where they are not. In both situations I hadn't explained the rules ahead of time. I just assumed they knew better. You know what assuming does! Mostly just makes me look dumb! That being said, it's impossible to anticipate what our kids are going to do at all times. Many rules will need to be explained on the spot with teachable moments like these. But there are plenty of stressful times in our day that can be avoided if we simply sit down with our children, lay out the rules in advance, and have a plan in place.

This is one of those situations. We have an hour each day at our house that I lovingly call "the witching hour." From 5:00 to 6:00 p.m. almost every day, without fail, my kids turn into something very unpleasant. It doesn't matter if they've had the best day ever and acted like perfectly behaved children up to that point, the devil inhabits their bodies during this hour and our entire day heads south. This is the hour leading up to dinnertime, when I am trying to cook. My husband generally arrives home at 6:00 p.m., and that's when we sit down to eat dinner as a family. So, he's not home to help during this "special" hour.

Since I am cooking during this hour, my full, undivided attention is not on my children. They are beginning to get tired at this point in the day, and they are getting hungry. Almost every day my husband would arrive home and the house would again be a disaster (although it was clean prior to this hour), the kids would usually be crying, fighting, or in some sort of trouble, and I was generally either in tears, angry, or had just given up on the children altogether. It was a vicious, vicious cycle, and it was showing no signs of improvement.

Something drastic had to be done, or we were going to start ordering pizza every night to save me from having to cook. Oh, did I mention I absolutely *hate* cooking? It doesn't matter what I am making or how many times I've made it in the past, I will find a way to ruin something every single night at dinner. I might possibly be the worst cook on planet Earth. That is why I hate cooking. So, naturally, cooking dinner puts me in a bad mood every day anyway.

In an attempt to stop the madness, I sat down with the two older boys, and we developed a plan. I gave them a list of activities they were allowed to do during that hour, and I specifically explained what they were not allowed to do during that hour. I used this example: I showed them all the dishes in the sink. I asked them how many of those dishes *I* had used. They answered that I had only used a plate, a cup, and a fork, yet there were at least fifteen other dishes in the sink. I asked the boys who the other dishes belonged to, and they named our other family members.

So I asked them, "Who washes all these dishes?"

They responded, "Mommy washes all of them."

I asked the boys if it was fair that *I* had to wash all the dishes even though I had not used all of them. They understood the point and said no. So I explained that, as a family, even if we didn't make the mess, or it's not our responsibility, we should still pitch in and help where we are needed. It takes everyone in the family to run a household, and we all have to help out and do our part.

Why did I illustrate this to the boys? Because not only did I need them to stay out of trouble and behave during that hour while I cooked, but I also needed them to help me keep an eye on Logan and keep him out of trouble. I couldn't get dinner made while Logan was constantly being "Captain Unhelpful" in the kitchen, and while the other boys were causing mischief in other parts of the house. I was being interrupted every few minutes to resolve some sort of conflict (which I'm going to go on record stating that that's why I mess up every meal, although my cooking has not improved since we came up with a plan).

So now the boys know exactly what activities they are allowed to do during that hour, and they almost always do a really good job of keeping Logan entertained and busy as well. It was simply a matter of laying out the rules and expectations in advance, and the behavior improved almost immediately. They certainly aren't perfect, and we still have days where our plan of action isn't effective, but overall this has taken one of the most stressful times of my day and transformed it into a much more pleasant and positive experience.

Maintain Your Rules in Public

Have you ever been at the grocery store and heard a toddler or young child screaming at his or her parents for candy? I know I've seen it many times. It may even have been your child one time or another. I know mine have done it to me at least once or twice. And many times, the parents give in and get the candy simply to keep the child quiet and keep the scene from escalating.

In the moment it seems like a great idea. You keep the peace, your child quiets down, and all the strangers stop staring at you and judging you and your parenting. But what do you suppose is going to happen the next time they go to the store? I would guess that nine times out of ten the situation will repeat itself. Eventually, the child will learn to demand bigger and better things. Once he or she figures out that you will give him or her candy for screaming simply to keep the child quiet, the child will ask for toys or electronics or whatever else is on his or her wish list. By giving in to the small things, you are creating a cycle that will become very difficult to break.

I've experienced a similar situation—not candy in the grocery store but equally difficult. For Christmas one year, my family took a trip to a cabin at Broken Bow Lake in southern Oklahoma. This was the same trip where we lost power due to the snowstorm. We were staying at the cabin for five days. Something you should know about my family is that we like to eat! We're a typical southern family. When we plan a vacation, the food menu is the first thing we make sure to get in place. Then we plan the rest of the activities around our meals. It's sad, I know. And you can be assured that there was a dessert planned for every evening after dinner. We didn't want to let Luke down! However, we never allow our boys to have dessert unless they eat their dinner first. This has been a longstanding rule in our house.

On the first evening in the cabin, we ate spaghetti and meatballs and salad for dinner. Luke ate all his salad and spaghetti with no problem as usual. But when it comes to dinner, Eli fights us almost every single night. If we're not having pancakes or pizza for dinner, he's not interested. We were prepared, and sure enough, he took two bites and asked if he could be finished. We explained very clearly that if he didn't eat his dinner, he wouldn't be allowed to have dessert. He said he was fine with that, and we excused him from the table. This is very normal for him.

About half an hour later, we began to serve dessert. And who do you think came into the kitchen with his big brown eyes looking so sad at us and asking if he could please just have a little bite of dessert? In that moment, we failed Parenting 101 as we talked ourselves into breaking our own rule. My husband and I looked at Eli's sad little face and began making excuses: *It is Christmastime. We are on vacation. Everyone else will be eating dessert in front of him. We don't want to make everyone else feel bad having to tell him no when he asks them for dessert. We don't want to look like really mean parents.* So we gave in and gave him dessert. And we paid dearly for that decision for the rest of the week.

Can you even guess what might have happened the next night? Yep, you guessed it. Eli fought with us about eating his dinner, ultimately ate two or three bites, and then was excused from the table again, stating he was fine not having dessert. Later that evening when dessert was served, he showed up, big brown eyes in place, begging for dessert again. When we told him no, he immediately began to whine and argue that we gave him dessert the night before and he hadn't eaten all his dinner then either. This continued every night while we were at the cabin and became extremely exhausting as the days wore on and the arguments grew longer and uglier.

Prior to this vacation, we had never given in to this rule regarding dessert. When it came time for a family gathering and dessert was served, Eli never argued with us about it. He knew the rule was set in stone, and we weren't planning to budge. But once we caved, even if it was only one time, he found a chink in the armor. He figured out that we were prone to change the rules when we are in public or at family gatherings. So he proceeded to see what other rules we might be willing to bend in those situations. We had created a monster. It only took one time, and we had set a pattern in motion.

It may seem harmless to give in the first time. It may resolve the situation in the moment. But ultimately, giving in to your child in public situations creates patterns that are very difficult to break. Our children are much smarter than we often give them credit for. They glean information from every situation and generally save it in their brains to use against us at a later time. Save yourself the trouble of having to break a bad habit later by not starting one in the first place.

Chapter 8

Speak Love into Them

Don't use foul or abusive language. Let everything you say be good and helpful, so that your words will be an encouragement to those who hear them.—Ephesians 4:29 (NLT)

When Luke started kindergarten, we were so excited about this new chapter. He was going to make new friends, learn a lot, and have fun. It was going to be such a positive experience that would instill in him a love for school from the very beginning.

Never could we have imagined that he would experience some of the things he did that year. He came home saying lots of new words and phrases that we did not allow in our home. He came home asking to watch certain movies or television shows that we did not allow in our home. We heard the phrase that every parent dreads and despises: "But (insert any particular name here) mom lets him do that. Why can't I?"

But the worst experience from Luke's kindergarten year was when he met a little girl in his class who tainted his budding self-esteem. I'm going to change the names to protect the innocent (or guilty) in this situation. I'll call her Kayla. Kayla was apparently really pretty. All of the boys in the class spoke of this often, and they all had quite the little kindergarten crush on her. She seemingly knew this about herself as well, if you know what I mean. She was also quite bossy and shared her opinions freely. But because she was so pretty and "popular," she also had a lot of influence over her peers.

Luke went to school one morning wearing his very favorite pair of athletic pants. He loved these pants because they were soft and comfortable. Remember, Luke is very much into his clothes, and he selected this particular outfit with lots of thought. That morning, he walked into the classroom and sat down next to Kayla. Without missing a beat, she looked right at him and said, "Those pants make you look fat."

Something you should know about Luke (really, all of my sons): he is very tall and skinny. From birth, his height on the growth charts has been around the ninety-fifth percentile and his weight around the third percentile. He has absolutely no body fat whatsoever. My sister often jokes with me about whether or not I actually feed him, because you can literally see his ribs sticking out. Trust me though, that kid can eat! He eats more than I do at most of our meals, so don't worry. I do feed him.

Keeping all of that in mind, this comment from little Kayla was out of left field. When Luke came home that day, he said nothing to us about Kayla's comment. In fact, he said nothing for about two weeks. I don't think he ever would have said anything about it had we not pressured it out of him.

Two weeks after she said that, I was laying out his clothes one evening for school the following day. And can you guess which pants I laid out? Yep, his "favorite" athletic pants. I was so excited because I knew we were not going to have a fight about his clothes that night, since he loved them so much. I couldn't have been more wrong. Once he spotted them, he told me, "I hate those pants."

I'm sure my mouth fell open at that moment from the shock. I immediately questioned him. "Why don't you like these pants anymore? They used to be your favorite. What changed that you no longer like them?"

He evaded every one of my questions until he finally got tired of them. Then he told me what Kayla had said. I was absolutely heartbroken that a little girl would say something so hurtful. I knew from my experience in school that kids can be mean, but I was floored that this was already starting in kindergarten. Kids should never have to deal with that, much less at five years old.

My husband and I sat down with Luke for a very long time and tried to discuss the situation with him. We explained that he should not care what others think of or say to him but that he should only care what he thinks. We reminded him of how much he loved those pants, and he should wear them if he loves them and not be bothered by what Kayla thinks. It didn't matter how many ways we explained it, we were not getting through. We haven't been able to get him to wear those pants since.

I realize we're just talking about a pair of pants here. But what happened runs much deeper than what you see on the surface. I think Luke really believed he was fat simply because Kayla told him he was. It didn't matter how many people told him he wasn't, he only remembered the one person who said he was.

I think this is so true of most people. I know it's true for me, especially. My husband can tell me every single day that he thinks I'm a great mom. But when I get that annoyed look or snide comment under her breath from another mom when my kids aren't behaving in public, I feel judged. Then I begin to label myself as a bad mom. I ignore the daily positive reinforcements that I receive, and I focus on the one negative comment or look that I get. It's quite ridiculous when you think about it logically. But that's the problem with emotions—they are never really logical.

The same is true for our kids. Particularly in school, they are going to have some negative comments fired their way. Other kids are going to be mean to them. Heaven forbid, they may have teachers who make them feel inadequate.

Your voice might be the only one they hear that makes them feel special. Your voice might be the only one they hear that makes them feel capable. Your voice might be the only one they hear that helps them realize they can be successful. Your voice might be the only one they hear that makes them feel loved.

Speak love into their lives every single day, and do it as many times a day as you are able. Your voice needs to be louder than all the other voices they hear at school or church or on their sports team or wherever they go. Your voice needs to be heard more frequently so it can outweigh all of the negative they might receive.

Be intentional about how you speak to your children and what you speak into their lives. Tell them every single day how much you love them. Tell them how important they are to you. Help them see that they matter and that God has a perfect purpose for their lives. You might be the only person they hear these things from, and you need to ensure that they believe it. Self-esteem matters as a child, and it follows you into adulthood. If you have a healthy self-esteem that was fed lots of positive reinforcements from your parents, I truly believe you will become a more successful adult. You have to believe in yourself if you are going to achieve your goals. Start feeding your children's self-esteems now, so they can grow into successful adults.

Chapter 9

Take "Me" Moments Every Single Day

The apostles returned to Jesus from their ministry tour and told him all they had done and taught. Then Jesus said, "Let's go off by ourselves to a quiet place and rest a while." He said this because there were so many people coming and going that Jesus and his apostles didn't even have time to eat. So they left by boat for a quiet place, where they could be alone.—Mark 6:30–32 (NLT)

I laugh at how ridiculous this sounds, but my two favorite times of each day are when I lay my head down on my pillow at night to go to sleep and when I sit down to drink my morning coffee and read my Bible each morning. Sleep and coffee! Seriously, my two favorite things in life (aside from my family and friends, of course!). Now don't get me wrong, I love waking up and seeing my husband's face next to me every day. I love my morning cuddles with my little Logan. I love breakfast giggles with my two older boys. I love dinnertime as a family. There are so many times in my day where I feel blessed beyond measure. But the reason I love my sleep and coffee time the most is because those are the two times each day where I am almost always guaranteed peace and quiet.

I have learned this about myself over the years: I am a person who loves calm and orderliness. When things are chaotic, I feel frazzled. When I feel frazzled, my emotions are on edge. And when my emotions are on edge, I tend to have emotional breakdowns or emotional outbursts depending on the situation. I need calm in my life.

Now, it seems great that I've figured this out about myself. It's important to understand what triggers your emotional overloads. But here's the problem. God gave me three ridiculously active boys. My boys don't even understand the words "calm" or "peace," much less are they able to put those words into practice. There are very few moments in my day where there is peace. Most days, Luke and Eli begin fighting the second their little feet hit the floor each morning. Logan starts throwing his special tantrums or his "helpfulness" as soon as he wakes each morning. My living room goes from picture-perfect cleanliness to looking like a tornado tore through it within half an hour of the boys waking up. My kitchen looks like a bomb went off in it following every single meal or snack throughout my day. And on and on and on. There is no peace. There is no calm. There is no order. There is only utter chaos almost all day.

So that's why sleep and coffee are my two favorite times of the day. When I lay my head down to go to sleep each evening, I melt into my pillow and relish in the fact that no one needs me at that moment. There is no fighting that I have to break up. There are no temper tantrums. There is nothing to clean up. I can simply lay my head down and drift off to sleep. It is so peaceful. I may be awakened at some point during the night, but at least at that moment it is sheer peace.

I don't know about you, but I can usually be nice, calm, and composed until around 7:00 p.m. each day. I likely will have had an entire day where I didn't yell at my kids, where I didn't lose my temper, where I did fun arts and crafts with my kids, where I made them some sort of special treat, etc. Then around 7:00 p.m.

each evening, something happens. I've expended all my energy, all my "fun" mommy moments, all my patience, and I can no longer compose myself. I've had enough. If my kids behave from that point until bedtime, then we can usually all survive the evening intact. But when they are rotten after 7:00 p.m., it's not pretty for anyone involved. So after a full night of sleep, I'm usually in a better place.

That's why my other favorite time of the day is my morning coffee and Bible reading time. I generally attempt to get up and get showered and ready before my kids wake up for the day, and I leave myself about thirty minutes for my coffee and Bible reading. During this time, my husband is generally gone for the day, my kids are still sleeping, and my house is completely quiet. I sit in my perfectly cleaned living room, drink my coffee, spend time with God, and read my Bible in pure peace and quiet. I love it! Again, no one needs me at that moment. There is no fighting happening that I have to break up. There are no temper tantrums. There is nothing to clean up. I can simply sit there, enjoy my coffee, and spend time with God.

Having that time with God each morning in the complete quiet gives me so much perspective. I am able to reflect on my life and truly appreciate everything God has blessed me with. I start out my morning prayer time each day by thanking God for my husband, my boys, my extended family, my home, and anything else that is on my mind. That puts me in the proper mindset for the day. When I thank God for my kids, in particular, it reminds me of everything I love about them. That helps me start the day off on a positive note, and it makes me a much better mom.

You may not enjoy coffee and sleep as much as I do. Maybe you prefer bubble baths. Maybe you love to read. Maybe watching television or a good movie is something you enjoy. Perhaps having a glass of wine on your patio in the evening sounds nice to you. Or how about a quiet walk through your neighborhood? It is so important to find at least one activity that you enjoy doing, and make sure you do it every single day. Find at least five to ten minutes in your day, whenever that may be, and enjoy some time to yourself. If you work, you may have to do that during your lunch break, or before you go pick your kids up from day care or school. If you stay home, you may need to utilize naptime. After the kids go to bed each evening is a good time to take advantage of as well if you're able.

Regardless of the activity or when you choose to do it, make sure you take some time for yourself each day. It is so important to have something to look forward to doing. And it is equally important to have time each day where you are uninterrupted by your kids, work, spouse, etc., so you can focus on yourself. You will be a much better parent if you take a little time for yourself each day.

Chapter 10

Choose Your Battles

And now, dear brothers and sisters, one final thing. Fix your thoughts on what is true, and honorable, and right, and pure, and lovely, and admirable. Think about things that are excellent and worthy of praise.—Philippians 4:8 (NLT)

We've all heard "choose your battles" before, but what does it really look like in parenting? As parents, we make hundreds of small decisions every day regarding our children, such as what they will wear, what they will eat, what activities they will participate in, where they will go, etc. The decisions begin the moment they wake and don't end until they go to bed, and oftentimes we are still making decisions for them while they are sleeping.

As our children grow into toddlers, they crave independence. That craving really never stops as they grow into elementary-school-age students, and then into middle school, high school, college, and even into adulthood. Independence is something we all crave. With our children, this often creates a struggle. We are ultimately the authority figure in the house that God has put in charge, but our children desire to be in charge of themselves. In order to combat this struggle for independence, I've found the answer in giving my kids choices. The younger they are, the fewer choices they should have. As they age, kids should receive more choices and the ability to make more decisions for themselves. However, all of the choices should be within the guidelines you, as a parent, have set forth.

As toddlers, their choices may be as simple as choosing between cereal or oatmeal for breakfast. Never leave it open-ended and ask a toddler, "What would you like for breakfast?" When you do that, they'll likely ask for ice cream or cookies. Then you're left telling them no when you were supposedly giving them a choice. This will defeat the purpose of giving them a little bit of independence.

I wish I could remember who said this, but my memory seems to be fading as I get older (or maybe I'm just losing my mind since having kids!). Someone once told me, "Tell your kids yes as often as you can, but when you say no, you need to mean it." I am a proponent of using the word no. I know lots of parenting experts who will tell you it's not a good idea. They may be correct. I'm not a doctor, nor do I claim to be a parenting expert. I simply know what has worked for my kids. I try to reserve telling my kids no in situations where it really matters or where I have a good reason to say no. Otherwise I try to say yes as often as I'm able. When you leave a question open-ended while offering a choice to a toddler, or even an older child or teenager, you are forced to tell them no oftentimes because they don't always have the ability to keep their decisions within reason. Save yourself some trouble and offer them choices when letting them make a decision. They will enjoy the freedom of making a choice, and the decision will be within the guidelines you have set forth. It's a win-win for everyone! I personally like those odds!

When your kids get a little older, increase their choices and give them a bit more freedom. You might ask them, "What activity would you like to do this weekend?" You can still give them a few, possibly three or four rather than only two specific choices, or you can leave it open-ended depending on the type of child you have. If you have a child who seems to generally make responsible decisions, this may be the type of child who does not need as many limits put on him or her. If your child is the opposite, then invoke more limits.

It may take some time to test the waters and see what type of child you have. When I started teaching, a fellow teacher said to me, "Don't let the kids see you smile until Christmas." What she was trying to tell me was that I needed to start out the school year being really tough and strict with my rules. Once I had my students in a good routine and they were behaving fairly well, then I could loosen the reins a little and allow them more freedom. I believe the same is true in parenting and allowing your children to make decisions. Start out slowly, and then give them more and more freedom to make decisions as they've shown you they can handle it.

However, don't feel defeated or lose hope if you're having to backtrack and reel your kids back in from having too much freedom. It's not the end of the world. I promise! Jesus has not come back yet. I would have seen him! Remember, tomorrow is a new day. Start fresh. Have a family meeting with your kids, and lay out the new rules and expectations. Sure, they'll fight you for several days, possibly even weeks, about not having as much freedom. But eventually, with lots of consistency, they'll conform.

My oldest son is very fashion-minded. Clothes are important to him, to say the least. I often laugh as I think about this, because I always assumed boys couldn't care less about their clothes. Apparently, I was wrong. What's new? One of our biggest battles every single morning used to be what he was going to wear. I knew it was coming each day, so I would have to brace myself for the impact and prepare for battle as I entered his room each morning. It was ugly! There was generally lots of yelling involved (on both our parts), sometimes tears were shed, and even doors were slammed at times. Tempers would flair.

I want my children to look nice and for their clothes to match. My children are a reflection of me. If they don't look nice, I assume everyone will judge me. That's probably not the case, nor does it matter if they do, but nonetheless, it's important to me.

Oftentimes what my son thinks is a matching outfit is far from it. It would embarrass me to let him leave the house in some of the outfits he chooses. This fighting each morning went on for a long, hard year. To say I was sick and tired of it was an understatement! In order to eliminate this battle, I came up with a few solutions. First, we started laying Luke's clothes out the night before. This helped alleviate stress in the morning when we were in a hurry. We discussed his clothing the night before when we had more time, so it wasn't during the rush to get to school and work when the stress level is already elevated. The second thing I did was ask for his input but let him know that I made the final decision. I might ask him which shirt he would like to wear, but I would choose his pants to ensure that they matched. That helped him feel more involved in the decision-making process. And finally, I allowed him to choose whatever clothes he wanted to wear on Saturdays and during the summer when I knew we weren't going anywhere or it didn't matter. That gave him the freedom to choose whatever he wanted at least one day each week. I often cringe when he walks downstairs on Saturday morning and I see the choice he's made. He usually looks quite ridiculous (by my standards). Most of the time, his clothes are mismatched. He likes to match oranges with reds, cowboy boots with shorts, and nice sweaters with sweatpants to name a few. But he's happy and I get to be happy with his clothes when it matters to me.

In that situation, I chose my battle regarding what he wore to school but not fighting what he wore on Saturdays and during the summer. By deciding what was important, it completely eliminated the fighting.

I choose my battles almost daily with all my boys. There are certain cabinets I don't want Logan, our one-year-old, to get into, so we added locks for his safety. But other cabinets that don't contain hazards we leave unlocked. This keeps him from getting very frustrated when I'm cooking dinner and he wants to play at my feet. I chose to allow entry into certain cabinets, even though I hate cleaning up the mess, in order to keep him happy while I'm busy cooking.

If you try to control your kids and dig your heels in on every issue, they'll rebel every chance they get. Choose the battles that really matter to you, and you will have much less arguing in your home. But be cautious, as there are certain things that are so important that you should not compromise. In our home, church is one of those things. We all go as a family, and that will not be a choice as the boys get older. It is important to us, and we feel it will truly impact the lives of our children, so we will not give the boys an option or compromise in any way regarding whether they attend. When they are in college and entering adulthood, we pray they will continue to attend church because we instilled the value of going at such a young age.

Choose what matters, but allow them some age-appropriate freedom in situations that are less important. It will make your home a more peaceful place.

Chapter 11

It Can Wait; Play Every Day

This is the day the Lord has made. We will rejoice and be glad in it.—Psalm 118:24 (NLT)

Y ou now know that I like to have my home and my life neat and organized. I have a schedule that includes cooking, housework, errands, etc. Crossing things off my to-do list gives me great satisfaction! Many times I get caught up in my to-do list and forget about the really important things in life.

I was a working mom for five years. Our family lives in a suburb of Dallas, so my commute each day took around twenty-five minutes each way. I woke my kids with just enough time to get them dressed, brush their teeth, and throw them in the car in the mornings. It was always a hectic, crazy, mad dash to get out of the door on time. Then we would drive the twenty-five minutes to their preschool where I would drop them off, always rushed, with very little time to get them properly settled into their classrooms.

After work, the crazy would start all over again. I would pick my boys up in the evenings, reverse the commute, and get home with just enough time to cook dinner, feed them, bathe them, and get them to bed. Again, a crazy, hectic, mad dash. My husband and I felt like we were running a never-ending race. As you can imagine, this did not leave us with very much time to spend with our boys during the week. To make matters worse, the weekends were spent trying to cram in as much housework, yard work, and projects around the house as we could get in. We really didn't spend much time with our children. I often found myself asking, "Is this how God intended for my life to be?"

Through much prayer and lots of anxiety, my husband and I made the decision for me to quit my job and stay home with our children. Our hope was that we could change the course of our lives and our children's lives by investing time and energy in them that they'd never had prior to this. In this economy, that seemed like a crazy decision. I mean, our nation was in a recession. I was a teacher, and there were literally thousands of unemployed teachers in our city looking for jobs that were not available, nor would they be available anytime in the near future. Who would possibly give up a secure and stable job at this time? But we knew God was prompting us to take this action, so we stepped out with blind faith and went for it.

I had so many doubts. Could we make this work financially? What happens if it doesn't work? Is there any chance of getting my job back or even any teaching job? Do I even like my kids enough to stay home with them? Don't judge me! I really asked myself that question. I questioned my ability to be a good stay-at-home mom. I knew myself well enough to know that I'm not one of those Suzie Homemakers who knits my kids' sweaters, makes homemade baby food (or homemade marshmallows like my mother-in-law; that woman is incredible), and has a perfectly clean house with clean, lovable children waiting for my husband when he gets home from work. I also asked myself questions like, would I resent my husband for not being home while I'm home with the kids? Would I get lonely? Would I turn into one of those *Desperate Housewives*?

There were so many doubts and questions going through my mind during this time. But God kept reminding me that he was in control and would not have told me to do something he couldn't help me through. I had to hold on to the truth that I was being obedient, so he would use this for my good. I did not want to be like the Israelites in the Old Testament who walked in the wilderness for forty years because they had not been obedient. Joshua 5:6 says, "The Israelites had moved about in the wilderness forty years until all the men who were of military age when they left Egypt had died, since they had not obeyed the Lord. For the Lord had sworn to them that they would not see the land he had solemnly promised their ancestors to give us, a land flowing with milk and honey" (NIV). My husband and I knew that we wanted our family to live in the "promised land" that God had prepared for us. I was scared, but I knew we would continue walking in the never-ending "wilderness" we were in if we were not obedient.

Like I said, it was a leap of faith. We took it. I'd love to say we never looked back, but those doubts continued to come. They still come at times when my boys are having an exceptionally rough day and I'm at my wit's end. I didn't title this book *My Kids Are Trying to Kill Me* for no reason! Those doubts still come at times when my husband and I sit down to look at our budget, and the money just isn't there. The doubts still come. But when they do, I silence them by quoting that scripture above. I know I am walking in obedience. I know it won't be easy all the time, as it was not for the Israelites. But, I know God will give our family our "promised land" if we continue to obey his Word and his plan for our lives.

One of the main reasons for my quitting my job was that we wanted a better quality of life for our family. We had visions of sugarplums dancing in our heads. No, wait, wrong story! We had visions of weekends spent playing in the yard with our kids rather than working. We had visions of family outings together every weekend. We had visions of picnics at the park as a family. You get the picture. We thought we would have an infinite amount of free time when I quit my job. We envisioned that I would have all of the housework done, the bills paid, and all the daily duties of running a house completed during the week, so we would have time for those things that were so important to us. We wanted our children to grow up knowing their parents were always around and never too busy for them.

What I quickly discovered is that being a stay-at-home mom is just as busy as being a working mom. I was spending my days running around like a crazy person trying to take care of the kids, come up with fun activities for them, teach the two younger boys preschool lessons since they weren't going to be in preschool anymore, clean the house, pay the bills, help my kindergartener with his homework, pack his lunch, etc. There simply was not enough time in the day to fit all that in. I was feeling frustrated and defeated. This was supposed to be my job now, and I was failing miserably. I had to figure something out and fast. I was drowning. And to add to the frustration, our financial situation was tight. We were struggling to stay within our budget each month. I began asking myself if I had made the right decision. The doubts flooded back into my mind on a daily basis.

Again, through crazy amounts of prayer and listening to the voice of God, he reminded me why we had made the decision for me to stay home. Keeping my house in pristine condition and making sure my life was in perfect order was not what was important in life. God reminded me that I needed to make sure to spend time each day playing with my children. That is what truly matters in life and what they will remember when they are adults. The housework and other chores can wait. I made a decision to get done what I could each day and do the best job I could possibly do. But I decided not to put so much pressure on myself to have everything perfect and in order. I now remind myself daily that "it can wait." Whatever chores you have to do, bills you have to pay, etc., are nothing compared to the importance of spending time each day playing with your children. The time you invest in your children during the short time you have them in your home will help shape them into the adults they will become. Invest your time wisely. Make them feel important.

All that being said, I find it important to mention that spending time with your kids doesn't count for anything if it's not quality time. Oh, how it pains me to admit this, but I am so guilty of spending time with my kids, but not really spending time with them. The main culprit for me … technology. My iPhone has been the biggest source of the problem for me. I will sit up on the floor of the playroom with my children while they are playing, and I will be playing games on my phone, or checking my Facebook page, or checking my e-mail, or countless other activities on my phone.

I don't know if it was God, or if Logan was just really annoyed with me, but I got the message loud and clear one day while I was sitting on the floor of the playroom *not* playing with my kids. I had received a text message, so I pulled out my phone to return the text. Then I noticed I had some new notifications on Facebook, so I checked those. Then I was tempted to see if I could pass the next level of Candy Crush Saga, the most addicting game on the planet! One thing led to another, and I had had my phone out for about fifteen minutes. Since I wasn't paying any attention to my kids, I didn't notice that Logan, sixteen months old at the time, was standing over me watching me play my game. He reached down very innocently, grabbed my phone out of my hand, and took off running at a full sprint. I watched in horror as he raced toward the railing above the stairs and proceeded to throw my phone over. Time seemed to move in slow motion at that moment. I jumped off the floor as quickly as I could and ran after him, but it was no use. There was nothing I could do except watch the phone, once again in slow motion, as it sailed down. It crashed on the wood floor below with a crack! This might be a nice time to mention that my husband had just bought me that phone two months before this happened. This was not going to be a fun thing to explain to him, "Sorry, babe, I was busy playing Candy Crush rather than taking care of our children. Logan didn't like that, or maybe it was God who was trying to send me a message, so Logan threw my phone over the rail. Now, could you please buy me a new one?" Ugh!

As I looked at my phone lying on the floor below, I realized it had landed face down. I dreaded looking, but that meant there might be a chance it was not broken. I walked slowly down the stairs, praying all the way. To my surprise, the only thing that had broken was a tiny piece of plastic on the side of my phone cover. I have no idea how I got that lucky, but I was thankful. Now I had to digest the message that Logan had sent me loud and clear. If I was going to spend time with him, I *actually* needed to spend time with him.

Time spent with our children does not matter unless we pay attention to them, play with them, and get involved in their interests and activities. Kids are very smart. They know when we are distracted and our attention and focus is not on them. Show your kids that they matter. Put life on hold, and make sure to spend time each day playing with your children. There will always be work to do, chores to get done, and projects that need to be completed, but your children are only in your home for a short period. Use that time wisely. You will never look back and regret that your bathrooms weren't perfectly clean all the time, but you will regret if you miss out on valuable time that could have been spent with your children.

Chapter 12

One Activity at a Time

So be careful how you live. Don't live like fools, but like those who are wise. Make the most of every opportunity in these evil days. Don't act thoughtlessly, but understand what the Lord wants you to do.—Ephesians 5:15–17 (NLT)

When I was a working mom of three young boys, which was only a year ago, this was a typical day at our house. I would wake at 5:00 a.m., shower, and get myself ready for the day. It generally took me about an hour. At 6:00 I would wake Logan to drink a bottle and get him dressed for school. At 6:45 I would wake the other two boys, dress them, and brush their teeth. Then we would head downstairs, pack our lunches, and grab any supplies or projects we needed for the day, and we would all rush out the door for school and work by about 7:10. My commute was around twenty-five minutes, so we would arrive at the boys' preschool around 7:35. After unloading, dropping each boy off in his classrooms or the cafeteria for breakfast, and visiting with their teachers, it was generally close to 8:00. I have to be at work at 8:15, so I would quickly head to work to make it on time. Most days I would walk in the door at 8:15 on the dot with no time to spare. I would generally eat breakfast in the car or as soon as I got to work, and then the crazy day would begin. I was exhausted before I even began my work day. At this point, I had been up for more than three hours, the entire time was rushed and chaotic, and I hadn't even begun my workday. Wow!

Once I had survived the crazy workday of dealing with middle school kids, I would leave work around 4:45 p.m. and go pick the boys up from school. By the time I had gathered all of them with their belongings, visited with their teachers concerning their days, loaded them in the car, and arrived home, it was typically 6:00. I would try to find ways to keep the boys entertained (and keep them from killing each other) while I would frantically cook dinner. Since they hadn't seen me all day long, they desperately wanted my attention. This was attention I couldn't give them in my frantic struggle to get dinner cooked so we could stay on schedule.

We would all sit down to eat dinner around 6:30. I was always wishing for a wonderful family dinner together, where we discussed our days and enjoyed one another's company. Instead, there was typically lots of arguing and whining, because at this point, everyone was exhausted from a long day of school and work, there was a fight for my undivided attention, which I could not offer, and I didn't really want to talk or listen anyway since I was equally exhausted. After dinner, we would rush immediately upstairs for bath time, in order to get all three boys in bed by 7:30 or 8:00 p.m.

That's when our other chores would begin. On a normal evening, we would try to get a load of laundry done, clean the kitchen, make lunches for the following day, grade papers if I had brought any home from work that day, and try to make it to bed by 10:00 p.m. The following day was the same routine. We would do this day in and day out. This probably sounds very familiar to some of you. Once I quit my job to stay home, things did get quite a bit simpler, but we still had schedules to follow, bedtimes to make, etc.

With a schedule like that, which I believe many people have, where do you find time for activities for your children? It's very difficult to fit them in, but I believe having your children in an activity of some sort, such as dance, sports, crafts, music, whatever it may be, is very important. Children learn many valuable life skills from being involved in activities with their peers. However, I feel that it is important to limit each child to one activity at a time. With the busy schedules many of us keep, our lives could end up revolving around our children's activities if we're not careful.

My boys love to be outside. They would live outside if we would allow that. Now that they are a little older, I usually send them outside to play in the backyard whenever I need to cook a meal or during various other times when they are too wild to be in the house. When they go outside, it almost always goes something like this: Luke immediately starts thinking about what type of game they are going to play. He can't stand to just play. There always has to be some sort of game with rules to follow. (I *love* games, so I can't imagine where he gets that from!) After he decides on the game, he begins to explain to Eli how to play the game. He never consults Eli to see what he would like to do, or even if Eli wants to play a game with him. He simply assumes Eli will play and do whatever he wants. I can usually hear or see the situation unfolding, and I brace for the tattling and fighting that is about to occur. As he is explaining the rules of the game, Eli begins to do things to deliberately make Luke angry. For example, Eli will start doing the chicken dance while Luke is explaining the rules just because he knows it irritates Luke. Eventually, Luke will get angry and impatient with Eli and begin yelling at him. That's when the tattling and fighting begins. This same scene happens day after day at our house.

Although that is the typical scene and I've tried to intervene many times, I believe it is important to let it happen sometimes. When my boys are playing together, even if they are arguing, they are learning valuable life skills. They are learning things like using your imagination to create, listening to your peers, responding appropriately to your peers, problem-solving on your own, and so many other important skills you need to be a successful child and later a successful adult.

Many of these skills can and are taught during children's activities such as sports, dance, gymnastics, etc. I wholeheartedly believe children should be involved in activities throughout their childhood, and even into adulthood. Activities teach children tons of valuable life skills and, most importantly, social skills. I think it is equally important to allow children time to learn some of these skills on their own. Children have to have a balance between free time and structured activities. I believe it is very important to give them an opportunity for both.

Most, if not all, children's activities involve at least two meetings each week. That may be a practice and a game, two practices to get ready for a recital, or whatever it may be. Many involve more. When children are involved in more than one activity at a time, it takes up many of their weeknights, and that takes away the time they would normally be able to play and enjoy being kids in a non-structured environment.

Additionally, being involved in too many activities very much affects the family unit. Some of the issues I've noticed when my children are overcommitted is that it causes relational problems within the family, adds stress to the daily schedule, and causes unhealthy eating habits. These crazy schedules cause relational strain between a husband and wife because there is less time for communication and time spent together. It also strains the relationship between us and our children. There is little or no time to enjoy our kids and really spend valuable time with them. Being overcommitted adds stress to daily schedules as well by having to juggle dinner, siblings, appointments, etc. And we've noticed, at least with our family, that it causes unhealthy eating habits. We generally eat more fast food because it's easier and faster when we are trying to get from activity to activity in a hurry. There is never enough time to cook or even pack a healthy meal when we are constantly in a hurry or on the go.

My recommendation is to slow down and choose one activity at a time for each child. We let our boys choose the activity for that season, however long the season may be. When the season ends, the boys may continue with that activity or choose a different one. Your kids will still have the opportunity to try many different activities to see the one(s) that are right for them. And, more importantly, they will still have plenty of time to play and enjoy being kids.

You will still have days where you are running from work or school straight to practice and grabbing fast food for dinner on the way, particularly in a family with more than one child. However, I promise you will notice less stress on your daily schedule, will have better relationships within the family, and will enjoy a much healthier family unit when you limit your children to one activity at a time. You will hopefully have at least one night a week where you will be able to sit down together and eat dinner as a family and truly enjoy your time together. It is so important to teach your children balance in their lives, and it starts with activities when they are young. Set a good example for them, and they will follow your lead through their lives. Show your children the importance of family time, and don't let your family life revolve around your children's crazy schedules and activities.

Chapter 13

Laugh Every Day

*A cheerful heart is good medicine, but a broken spirit
saps a person's strength.*—Proverbs 17:22 (NLT)

I took Eli and Logan for their well-check appointments at their
pediatrician, who also happens to be my sister. The appointments
were scheduled for 10:00 a.m. The doctor's office was running a
little behind, plus my brother-in-law was at the office that day and
my boys love seeing him, the boys needed vaccines, etc. When all
was said and done, we didn't leave the office until noon. We were
thirty minutes from home, and I still had to get the boys fed and in
bed for naps.

I was a little stressed out, as I am quite a schedule-oriented
person. I'm always thinking ten steps ahead. If we get off our daily
schedule, it will throw meal and snack times off, and then dinner
and bedtime will fall behind. I'm seriously crazy when it comes to
keeping my kids on a schedule. In addition, I have learned from
experience that if we are in the car too close to Logan's naptime, he
will fall asleep in the car. You might be thinking, *What's the big deal
if he falls asleep in the car? It's not the end of the world.* Trust me, I get
it. But as I mentioned before, I'm crazy! It matters to me if Logan falls
asleep in the car because once he does, he thinks that's his only nap

for the day. It doesn't matter if he falls asleep for two minutes, five minutes, or forty-five minutes, he wakes up and thinks naptime is over. So I'm thinking in terms of the rest of the day here. With only a thirty-minute nap, the rest of the day will be quite unpleasant for us all, since Logan will be rather cranky.

Also, I usually hate to buy my kids fast food because we're on a strict budget since I've quit my job. Knowing we have food at home and spending money anyway really bothers me. I'm a bit of a cheapskate! But nonetheless, I made the decision to stop at McDonald's in order to speed up the process and try to keep some semblance of our regular schedule. McDonald's, the lunch of champions!

We grabbed our food, and I was feeling pretty good since Logan did not fall asleep on the way home. But I know I still have to get the boys fed and down for naps fast before everyone starts melting down from being overly tired. That being said, you can imagine I'm still a bit on edge.

In the midst of my stress, Eli asked me, "Mommy, did we get a toy with our meal?"

I said, "No, honey. I'm sorry. I didn't get you a *Happy* Meal this time."

That kid doesn't even miss a beat. With that mischievous little twinkle in his eye, he says, "Well, did you get me a *mad* meal, or an *angry* meal?" In that moment, all the stress disappeared as I burst out laughing at my little jokester! The fact that I stopped in the middle of the chaos and stress just to laugh at his silly joke made him the happiest kid in the world that day.

Now I realize what a crazy person I sound like. I know this situation was not the end of the world, and I seriously should not be stressing out over something as silly as deviating from our daily routine. Nonetheless, this is me, for better or worse. I'm not always sane! But it does illustrate my point rather well. Not only did laughing with my little guy in that moment make him feel amazing, it made me feel good! I'm no scientist or medical expert, but I've watched *Legally Blonde*. So I know for a fact that laughing is like exercising for your body, because you exert energy when you laugh. And exercising gives you endorphins, which make you happy. And "Happy people don't kill their husbands," as Elle Woods so intelligently deduces in the law practice! Okay, so maybe that was a stretch. But in all seriousness, when you laugh, it relieves much of the stress you are feeling. It makes you feel good. And it helps you be a better, more relaxed parent. When I laugh with my kids, I know I tend to snap at them less, I don't lose my temper as much, and I'm much less on edge. The real bonus is that they behave much better because they know they have my attention and they feel much more loved.

Here's another example of a time when laughing truly helped relieve my anxiety and defuse a stressful situation. It was summertime, and I had scheduled haircut appointments for my three boys. It's difficult to get an appointment for all three at the same time, but I had managed. I knew if they were all strapped into the chairs at the hair place at the exact same time, there was little they could do to cause trouble. That would give me at least twenty minutes of peace! Yes, I really think like that.

I changed Logan's diaper, put shoes on all the boys, and set Logan's infant carrier by the front door. I sat Logan down on the floor next to his carrier and asked Luke and Eli to go stand next to him while I gathered my purse and the diaper bag. I was ready to walk out the door and head to the haircut place, or so I thought.

I reached into my purse but couldn't find my keys. This is not unusual for me, as sometimes I absentmindedly lay them on the kitchen counter rather than putting them away in my purse. So I automatically looked there first. Not there. I continued searching some other common places I might have left them, but no such luck. Now the clock is ticking and we are getting close to our appointment time. As I was racking my brain about where the keys might be, I decided to call my mom. My mom and dad had been at our house a few days prior to this, and they had driven my car. I was confident she would know where to look. Plus, my mom is the most organized person I know. Even if she didn't know where they were, she would have fifteen ideas of places to check that I hadn't thought of. Yes, I'm thirty-two years old and I still need my mom for everything. Sad, right? And I was right, she had some great ideas. But I still couldn't find the keys.

At this point, I have torn apart several of the couch cushions thinking they might have fallen into the furniture; I have checked everywhere my mom suggested I look, I've even checked in the car, and I am now growing frantic. There is no way we are going to make our appointments on time, and now we are in danger of having to cancel them altogether. I see my twenty minutes of peace fleeting before my eyes!

I am getting ready to hang up the phone with my mom and give in to defeat, when I look up at my boys, whom I have been neglecting while frantically searching for my keys. I have learned over the years to never leave my children unattended for longer than about twenty minutes without some sort of visual. I had been looking for my keys for twenty-five minutes, so I was past my window.

Luke and Eli had gotten into the coat closet at the front door and located a scarf during this time. As I examined what was happening more closely, I realized to my dismay, they were twisting the scarf around Logan's arms and legs and were tying him to his car seat. At that moment I forgot I was on the phone with my mom, and I yelled across the room, "Boys, stop tying your brother up!" I feel like there are certain phrases I should never have to utter. That was one of them. But nonetheless, here I was yelling it to my children. What I had forgotten was that my mom was still on the phone. She immediately burst out laughing, which infectiously made me start laughing. Another stressful situation defused with laughter.

I called the hair place to cancel our appointments and continued looking. I finally found my car keys—three hours later!

After all that time, I remembered that it had been raining the previous Saturday, and I had been wearing my raincoat. I had absentmindedly stuck my keys into my coat pocket and hung the coat back in the closet.

I learned three very valuable lessons that day. 1. Always check your coat pockets first when you lose your keys. I have done this many times since this day, and it has paid off. 2. Hang the scarves up on a higher shelf so my children cannot reach them and use them for mischievous purposes. 3. You always feel better when you stop and laugh every single day. It releases stress and tension, it changes the attitudes and behaviors of your children, and it helps you enjoy life. Laugh often, especially with your kids.

Chapter 14

Invite Them Anyway

As Jesus and the disciples continued on their way to Jerusalem, they came to a certain village where a woman named Martha welcomed him into her home. Her sister, Mary, sat at the Lord's feet, listening to what he taught. But Martha was distracted by the big dinner she was preparing. She came to Jesus and said, "Lord, doesn't it seem unfair to you that my sister just sits here while I do all the work? Tell her to come and help me." But the Lord said to her, "My dear Martha, you are worried and upset over all these details! There is only one thing worth being concerned about. Mary has discovered it, and it will not be taken away from her."—Luke 10:38–42 (NLT)

When you walk into my house on any given day, you are bound to find toys scattered on the floor, wood chips and grass from the backyard tracked all throughout the house, dishes in the sink from our last meal, pee on the toilet (another thing that drives me insane with boys), etc. I seriously clean all day long, but I can't keep up with the mess these crazy boys make in our house. I once read that "cleaning a house with children in it is like trying to brush your teeth while eating Oreos." That could not be truer at my house. The only time I actually feel like I make a dent in the mess is when my boys are napping, or when they are in bed at night.

I've actually considered begging my husband to take the children to Grandma and Grandpa's house for a weekend just so I can clean the house from top to bottom. Then my entire house might be clean at the same time for the first time ever!

For a long time, I was embarrassed to have friends over because of the mess. I would wait until they invited us over to their house, or I would always suggest we get together at a restaurant, a park, or in a public place. It was just so difficult for me not to have a perfectly clean house. Because I wouldn't invite my friends over, many times I would miss out on quality time with them. As a mom, particularly now as a stay-at-home mom, this "adult" time is very important to me. I need that time with my friends to recharge, sometimes vent, laugh with them, share stories, etc. Life is so much better when you are surrounded by good friends.

I finally decided to get over myself, stop worrying so much, and just invite my friends over regardless of the condition of my house. This was a huge step for me. It may not be a big deal to some of you, but I think, particularly as women, we're always trying to impress each other. I always joke that everything is a competition with my boys (and I think the same with some men). However, I think women are fairly competitive as well. Oftentimes we just aren't as vocal about it. We are competing in terms of physical appearance, how well we parent our children, or how nice our house is—the list goes on and on. One significant way we, as women, try to impress each other is by striving to make our lives look perfectly put together and in order. At least that was true for me for a long time. I didn't want anyone to know my house was a mess or that I was a mess! As long as my image looked good from the outside, I was fine.

Once I stopped caring and took that step by inviting my friends over regardless of the state of my house, it was so freeing. I found out that my friends didn't even care. They loved me no matter how my house looked. I also found they were exactly like me! Their houses weren't clean either, nor were their lives perfect and in order. This opened up a whole new door for me. I learned how to be honest about my life and how I was feeling and to be more open with my friends. I was no longer trying to impress them and make everything appear perfect. If we as women (and I suppose some men; I hate to leave you out) would all open up and be honest with one another, we could live a much more relaxed and free life. Stop worrying about what everyone thinks of you. Be yourself. Be open and honest. And most importantly, enjoy your life and your much-needed time with your friends.

Chapter 15

There Is Value in the Struggle

And we know that God causes everything to work together
for the good of those who love God and are called according
to his purpose for them.—Romans 8:28 (NLT)

I love when things don't go my way. I love when something is a struggle. I love life's trials. I love when we don't have enough money to make it to the end of the month on our budget. I love it when my kids fight constantly. I love when my kids talk back to me and misbehave. I love when a virus infiltrates our house. I love when I've had a crazy day and my husband calls to tell me he's going to be home late that night. I love when my kids wake up at night because they've wet the bed or had a bad dream and I'm up during the night helping them.

Who's with me on these things? Do you love them too? Ha! Of course not! I don't know anyone who would say he or she loves any of those things I listed above. But what I want you to see is the importance and value of those things in shaping us into the people we are meant to be. I want you to think of one of the strongest (not physically, but emotionally) people you know. Picture him or her in your mind while I tell you a story. Think about the story of your "person" as I'm telling this one. I'm going to use the example of my parents. Here is the "Cliff's Notes" version of their lives.

My mom and dad met when they were thirteen and sixteen, respectively. They dated on and off for several years. When my mom was seventeen, and my dad was twenty, they found out they were pregnant with my sister. They were not yet married but quickly decided to get married. Expecting a child at seventeen, my mother did not have an opportunity to go to college. My dad went to college for a semester but did not get any further than that. Poor, with no help from their parents, they decided to move to another state after the birth of my sister. With no college education, they had very few opportunities available to them, so they both got a minimum-wage job working at a chicken plant. A couple of years later, they brought me into the world.

My parents continued to press forward and work hard to save money, until eventually they had enough money to move to another state and eventually purchase their first home. It was an uphill battle from the beginning, but they were determined. They continued to struggle financially for the next several years.

When I was around ten years old, my parents had saved enough money to put my dad through community college, and then on to a four-year university. Once he had a college education, other opportunities began to open up for him. Long story short, through hard work and determination, my parents are now some of the most successful people I know. They own multiple buildings, which they rent out, and two very successful businesses.

I know if you were to ask them today if they enjoyed the poor life with two young children, they would absolutely say no. They can tell you story after story of their struggles. I only shared a few of the highlights. But they would not be the amazing, strong, generous, and loving people they are today had they not gone through those struggles.

So when I am struggling with my kids, I always try to think of their story. When my husband and I are trying to stretch our money to make it to the end of the month, I think of their story. When my kids get sick and I am up with them at all hours of the night, I think of their story. I always remember that these trials and struggles are building me into the person God intends for me to be. God wants me to be generous, kind, loving, unselfish, humble, joyful, calm, caring, and so many other characteristics. God wants my life to reflect "the fruit of the Spirit," which is "love, joy, peace, forbearance, kindness, goodness, faithfulness, gentleness, and self-control" (Galatians 5:22–23 NIV). I can only become a loving person because God has shown me his love time and time again throughout the trials in my life. I can experience true joy because I've come out on the other side of some of my trials in life, and I know without a doubt that God brought me through them with his mighty hand, and that I experienced them for my good. I can be at peace in my life because I know God has every single detail of my life completely in his hands, and even in times of struggles, he is in control. I can become the person God wants me to become, but not without trials and struggles.

So rather than praying or wishing away your struggles in life, try embracing them. The Bible says in James 1:2–4, "Consider it pure joy, my brothers and sisters, whenever you face trials of many kinds, because you know that the testing of your faith produces perseverance. Let perseverance finish its work so that you may be mature and complete, not lacking anything" (NIV). I don't know about you, but I find it very difficult to "consider it pure joy" when I am in the midst of a struggle. However, I hold strong to the rest of that scripture. I don't want to be "lacking anything." I want to be "mature and complete." If I need to go through trials and struggles to achieve this, sign me up.

Remember that struggles make you stronger, more determined, more loving, and more generous, and they develop perseverance in you. I've seen it firsthand in the lives of my parents. I've seen it firsthand in my life. There is so much value in the struggle. Be thankful for every single challenge you face, as these challenges are shaping you into the amazing person God desires you to be. You will be complete, lacking nothing.

Chapter 16

Everything Is a Phase

For our present troubles are small and won't last very long.
Yet they produce for us a glory that vastly outweighs them
and will last forever!—2 Corinthians 4:17 (NLT)

I say this phrase to myself and my friends almost daily:
"Everything is a phase." And I truly mean it. As I look back over
the past six years of being a parent, I can vividly recall many times
where I thought, *I'm not going to survive this!* I can also remember
many times where my friends came to me asking for advice in certain
situations when they thought they weren't going to make it.

Starting as early as birth, when my babies were not sleeping
through the night, I felt like that would last forever. Now all three of
my kids sleep through the night (on most nights). As they grew into
toddlers and started throwing tantrums, I thought we would never
be able to go to a restaurant again. But I can start to see glimpses
of restaurants in my future as I see how my oldest is now behaving
in public. Then there's the "terrible twos" and the "horrible why
didn't anyone warn me threes." I've been through both those ages
with two of my boys, and I'm certainly not looking forward to
going through it again with the third child, but I now know I can
survive it.

Now that I've realized that everything children go through is a phase, it changes my perspective. Here are some practical tips for coping when you're in the midst of a phase. First, look at other's kids who are older than yours. Are they still exhibiting the behaviors you are seeing in your child? In most cases if they are not, your child probably won't be at that age either. That will help you to put a time frame on when your phase might end.

For example, Logan gets into absolutely everything. He wears me out. I put him into timeout, I find ways to baby-proof things, and I move things out of his reach. Nothing seems to work. I get so frustrated every day at redirecting him and disciplining him when nothing seems to change. To be honest, it's rather annoying. But in the midst of my frustration every day, I often have to stop and pray to keep my irritation from bubbling over into anger. What God reminds me while I'm praying through this each day is that it is a phase and will change with age. He reminds me to look at my other children, who are older, and my friends' children, who are older. My four- and six-year-old rarely get into things they are not supposed to. When I go to my friends' homes who have older children, or when they bring their children to my house, their kids are not digging through my cabinets, playing with the television remotes, unrolling the toilet paper rolls, or the many other things Logan does daily. This gives me so much hope and perspective. It is only a phase, and it will change with age.

Second, I often ask myself, "Is it likely that my child will still be exhibiting this behavior in high school or college?" For example, I might ask myself, "Will my son still be throwing his sippy-cup across the room when he's in high school?" Another bad habit Logan likes to do. Likely the answer is no. How many kids in high school or college are still throwing things at the dinner table? Probably none that you know of. If that's the case, however frustrating it may be in the moment, it is likely a phase and will end at some point. Sometimes the answer is yes when I ask that question. Here's one of those situations: "Will my son still be peeing all over the toilet and on the floor around the toilet when he is in high school and college?" The answer is most definitely yes because boys are disgusting. In that case, I know it's not a phase and I just completely give up on fighting that battle!

A third thing I do when my children are going through a phase that's wearing me out is to try to find the joy in the situation. I try to remember what I love about my kids at that age. When I was working full-time after my third son, Logan, was born and he still was not sleeping through the night, I remember being exhausted and miserable and thinking I wasn't going to survive that newborn stage a third time. Through much prayer, God reminded me to find joy in that situation. In James 1:2–3, the Bible says, "Consider it pure joy, my brothers and sisters, whenever you face trials of many kinds, because you know that the testing of your faith produces perseverance" (NIV). Can you tell I love that verse? So rather than being grumpy about getting up in the middle of the night, I chose to focus on the extra time I got to snuggle with Logan. With him being my last child, it made me appreciate that time so much more. I sat there during those long nights, snuggling him, pulling him closer, and thanking God for the blessing of that sweet boy.

Children will go through an infinite amount of phases as they grow into the adults they will become. They may go through a phase of sassing, spitting, slamming doors, poor choices in school, even more severe phases. It is our job as their parents to outlast them, coach them, and guide them through these phases to the best of our ability. Remember to find the joy in each stage of your children's lives, and your entire perspective will change and will alter the way you interact with your children.

Chapter 17

Be Honest

Obviously, I'm not trying to win the approval of people,
but of God. If pleasing people were my goal, I would
not be Christ's servant.—Galatians 1:10 (NLT)

This chapter is very difficult for me but so important for me to share. In sharing, I'm bearing my soul and uncovering some of my greatest insecurities. I have had self-esteem problems as long as I can remember. I have always been slightly overweight. I wore giant eighties-style glasses through most of my childhood (no, I will not include a picture for your laughter!). I always had some great friends, but I was never in the popular crowd. Even in college I never had the confidence to join a sorority or clubs until late in my college years. For some reason I've always felt like I'm not good enough, not cool enough, not popular enough, and not pretty enough. I'm certain some of you reading this can relate. Particularly women seem to deal with this more frequently than men in my experience.

As I became an adult, I thought surely this problem would improve. I mean, I'm not in high school anymore. There aren't the "cool" kids anymore. The dividing lines are gone, right? Then I became a mom. That took my insecurities to a whole new level. Now not only did I feel like I wasn't good enough, but now I wasn't good enough for my kids. I constantly began to worry that they were not going to turn out as well-rounded adults and it was all depending on me and my abilities as a mom. Wow! That was a lot of pressure!

I often used to compare myself to other moms: How has she had three kids and she's that skinny? How is she so calm in speaking to her children when I lose my temper with my kids every day? Why do her kids already know how to read going into kindergarten and mine doesn't? How does she have enough money to take her kids on fun vacations every year and we don't? Why are her kids so calm, polite, and well-behaved and mine aren't? I asked these questions and many others on a daily basis. I centered my life around comparing myself to others and how I never measured up to them.

My self-esteem was terrible, and it had a huge impact not only on myself but on my husband and kids. My husband would tell me I was beautiful or that I was a great mom, and I would just shrug him off. My mom, as well as my sister and others in my family would encourage me, but the voice in my head telling me I wasn't good enough was so much louder than the other voices. I was battling years of negative feelings about myself that I knew weren't going to change without a fight.

To compound the situation, technology seemed to make things more unbearable. Facebook was the worst. I would log on to the computer to check my Facebook and see posts from all these other moms about how adorable, wonderful, and successful their kids were. I absolutely love Facebook because it helps me keep in touch with my friends, but oftentimes I would log off feeling inadequate yet again.

About three years ago, I made a decision that would change the way I thought about myself and others. I decided I didn't like who I had become, and I hated myself for always wanting to be like everyone else. I believe God put this on my heart, and it is only through his strength that I have been able to get to the place I am in today. The decision I made was so simple, yet so powerful. I decided I was not going to live my life constantly caring what others think of me, but I was only going to care what God thinks of me. Simple, right? Sounds easy? I'll just wake up tomorrow and stop caring about the opinions of others and live a much happier life. Unfortunately, it wasn't that simple.

I started with small steps. The Bible says in Zechariah 4:10, "Do not despise these *small beginnings*, for the Lord rejoices to see the work begin" (NLT, emphasis added). So I began the work. I started by waking up each day and telling myself that God created me exactly as he wanted me to be and he loves me exactly as I am. If I were exactly like someone else, I could not fulfill my unique purpose God had given me to complete while here on earth. It was so difficult to believe for a very long time, but I repeated this mantra every single day until I actually believed it. Then I began telling myself that I don't care what others think of me but only what God thinks of me. Again, after an extended period of time, I began to believe it.

Then came the difficult part. I talked to others about my insecurities. I opened up to my closest friends about how I was feeling, about where I was failing as a wife, about where I was struggling as a mom, and about my insecurities with my physical appearance. Through admitting my struggles, I felt like a weight was lifted off my shoulders. I no longer felt like I was living in the dark, hiding how I was feeling all the time. And surprisingly enough, my friends began to open up to me about their struggles and insecurities. Even more surprising, I found that my friends shared the same emotions.

I truly believe Satan wants us to live in a dark place of isolation. He wants us to feel alone and insecure, as if we are the only one going through the struggles we face. He is the voice in our heads telling us we are not good enough. But when we step out of ourselves and share our problems with others, we receive a sense of freedom that can only come from God. When we open up to others, we receive the help and encouragement that we need from them, but even more importantly, we are able to help them through their struggles as well. It is so important to be honest about how you feel. Don't silently struggle through life. Rely on your family and friends to help you and encourage you along the way.

Chapter 18

Welcome Members of the Family

Children, obey your parents because you belong to the Lord, for this is the right thing to do. "Honor your father and mother." This is the first commandment with a promise: If you honor your father and mother, things will go well for you, and you will have a long life on the earth. Fathers, do not provoke your children to anger by the way you treat them. Rather, bring them up with the discipline and instruction that comes from the Lord.—Ephesians 6:1–4 (NLT)

In January 2007 I came home after a long day at work. I was exhausted. All I wanted to do was eat some dinner and go to bed. But what was the point? I hadn't been able to sleep in months since I was nine months pregnant with our first son, Luke. I was beyond uncomfortable, and I was still two weeks away from my due date. It felt like an eternity. Around 8:00 p.m. I started to have contractions. Within an hour, the contractions had moved to five-minute intervals, so we packed up our bags and headed to the hospital. Sure enough, I was in labor. All I could think was, why couldn't he have come in the morning after I'd at least had a few hours of sleep! But nonetheless, he was coming.

I was in labor for sixteen hours (twelve with no epidural) before he made his appearance in the world. At that point I had been awake for more than twenty-four hours. I was exhausted. This was supposed to be one of the happiest moments of my life, and all I wanted to do was sleep. I'm sure part of that was from the pain medicine, but man, was I tired!

That was only the beginning. If I thought I was tired after labor, I had no idea what was coming. My friend Kelly likes to remind me quite frequently of how ridiculous I was before I had kids. She had her first child before we had ours. When I was around eight months pregnant, she asked me what I was most looking forward to after I gave birth to Luke. She was expecting me to say something like a glass of wine. But in my ignorance, all I could think about was my lack of sleep from being so uncomfortable during this pregnancy. So I told her I was most looking forward to sleeping through the night again. She practically fell on the floor laughing hysterically at me. I didn't think she was ever going to stop. She knew the one thing about being a new parent that no one can possibly prepare you for. There will be *no sleep*. She had experienced it. And soon so would I.

We left the hospital after three days and brought our little miracle home. By day five of his life, he no longer seemed like a little miracle. He was waking up every two to three hours at night. He wasn't getting enough to eat, so he was extra fussy, and he wouldn't go back to sleep for hours once I fed him. I'm sure this scene sounds very familiar to most of you. There is really nothing like that new-parent feeling of exhaustion. You know you need to sleep so your body can heal and recover. You desperately want to sleep. But this precious little child doesn't want to sleep. You see no light at the end of the tunnel when you are in the midst of the situation. It feels so hopeless.

I vividly remember a conversation I had with my mom when Luke was about one week old. We had been out running several errands and it was nearing dinnertime. I was starving. We stopped to pick up fast food somewhere and headed home. About the time we got home, Luke woke up ready to eat. I struggled and struggled to feed him. After about forty-five minutes, we had him satisfied. At this point, I was beyond starving and now my food was cold. I literally sat there and started to sob. As I munched on my soggy, cold French fry, I said to my mom, "I'm never going to eat another warm meal again, am I?"

I know how ridiculous that sounds, but what I was really thinking was, *My life is so different now.* I seriously didn't know what I had gotten myself into, and I was afraid I was going to have to center everything in my life around this child. I was terrified I was never going to have time for me again.

After several months passed, things got easier, we got into a routine, and life settled down a little. I realized everything was going to be okay. I would survive a few cold meals, and I would get warm meals again in the future. Luke was sleeping around ten hours a night by the time he was three months old, so I was now getting a good amount of sleep again. Having children is a huge adjustment, but it doesn't have to completely change everything in your life. You will have to adjust your life in the beginning for a few months, but things will get back to normal.

My husband and I took a parenting class at our church prior to having Luke, to help prepare us for what was in store. One major point they preached was that your baby is a "welcome member of your family," but you are not to center your entire life around him or her. That point has really stuck with me over the past six years. We try as a family to plan and choose our events and activities according to the schedule that works best for our entire family unit. We don't allow our children to dictate how our weekends run or how our weeks will go. This one principle has helped our family tremendously over the years. It has allowed us to be a well-rounded family where we, the parents, decide what is best for our family and for our children.

My middle son, Eli, often asks for outrageous things just to see if I'll allow it. He's always testing the waters. Regularly, he'll ask for ice cream for breakfast, or if he can jump on the bed, or if he's allowed to drive without a seat belt. I often laugh at how crazy this child is, but he knows I'm not going to give in. He truly wants those things, but I know what's best for him. If I allowed him to have ice cream for breakfast every day just because he asked for it, what kind of parent would I be? My husband and I make the decisions in the house, because God has entrusted us with the job of raising these little boys, and he's shown us the best way to go about it. Proverbs 22:6 says, "Start children off on the way they should go, and even when they are old they will not turn from it" (NIV). If we allow our children to make the rules and decisions, we give up our control. When we do that, we are asking for chaos and trouble, and when they are older, they won't have a clear direction for their lives.

I believe the best way to keep balance in a family and not allow the children to run the show is to remember that children are "welcome members of the family." Don't allow them to come in and change your entire life and disrupt your family routine. God has given you the divine appointment to parent those children, and whether you believe it in every situation or not, you know what's best for your children. Rely on God and his perfect Word to guide you and lead you in raising your children his way. Don't allow your children to be in charge. You take charge of your family and see the amazing blessings God will pour into your family when you are walking in obedience and structuring your family the way he wants it to be.

Chapter 19

Bedtime Is a Must

Unless the Lord builds a house, the work of the builders is wasted. Unless the Lord protects a city, guarding it with sentries will do no good. It is useless for you to work so hard from early morning until late at night, anxiously *working for food to eat; for* God gives rest to his loved ones.—Psalm 127:1–2 (NLT, emphasis added)

P arenting is exhausting. It takes every bit of energy just to make it to my boys' bedtime each night. I've said it before: my kids have a limitless amount of energy. If I allow them to stay up until they get tired, I'm not sure they would ever go to bed. I can often see signs that they may be tired, such as arguing with each other, whining, or simply frequent meltdowns over very small things. But my children never slow down and get sleepy, so my boys have a fairly strict bedtime. Even if they are not tired at that moment, I feel it is important for them to be in bed and resting at that time. I'm no doctor, but I know how important it is for my kids to get a full ten to twelve hours of sleep each night. I see how their bodies and minds react when they don't get enough sleep.

Equally important is recuperating our minds and bodies each evening as parents. Kids need a set bedtime each night, in order for us as parents to get the rest we need as well. My husband and I don't go to bed right after our kids do; we generally stay up for a few hours after. That is our time to get a few chores completed, look at our budget together, plan activities, watch television, play games, or just visit with one another. It is so important as parents to have time away from as well as time with your kids. Bedtime is an important way to regularly have that time away from them. Whether you are married, or a single parent, you need this time each evening to rest from the activities of the day. I promise you will be a better parent when you take a little time for yourself and/or your spouse each day. You will be refreshed and ready to take on another day with your kids.

In order to establish this set bedtime, it is important to have a routine and stick to it each night. At our house we eat dinner and then immediately head upstairs. While the kids have quiet playtime in their playroom, my husband and I take turns giving baths, laying out clothes, and getting the boys ready for bed. Then we all sit down together as a family and read a Bible story. Following that, we send each child to his own separate room to wait for us to come tuck him in. We say an individual prayer with our boys while they are laying in bed, give bedtime kisses and hugs, turn off the light, close the door, and they go to sleep. They may not fall asleep immediately, but they know not to come out of their rooms once the door is closed. We do the exact same thing almost every night. If we don't deviate from the routine, then they generally won't either. Generally.

That being said, kids are still kids. When Eli turned four, he went through a bit of a defiant streak. This was super fun! My husband and I would go through our normal bedtime routine, and then we would close the door after putting him to bed. He would wait about twenty minutes, listening to make sure we had gone downstairs, and would come out of his room. He would always make up some excuse, and we would send him back. Sometimes he needed a drink of water. Other times it was a tissue to blow his nose. He even got really creative at times and would fake coughing and ask for medicine, or tell us he had a tummy ache and needed to go to the bathroom. He would come up with any reason he could think of to stay out of his room. I don't know if he thought he was missing out on some sort of fun we were having without him or what, but he was not backing down.

Since he was not backing down, we dug our heels in and refused to give in either. We knew we had to get this issue under control, even if it killed us. We threatened all sorts of consequences, and we carried them out. The only problem with that strategy is that consequences don't often deter our little Eli. We have yet to come up with a consequence that bothers him, and we have tried them all! We've asked all of our friends, family members, even Google. We've read parenting books regarding raising children, setting boundaries, positive discipline, specifically raising boys, etc. Finally he seemed to get tired of our anger and all of the consequences, so he gave up the fight. Or so we thought!

It took us about a week to realize it, but Eli had not been compliant in going to bed when we closed the door as we had previously thought. Rather than getting out of his bed and coming to us with excuses as to why he needed out of his room, he got really sneaky about it. That's when we nicknamed him our little ninja. He would come out of his room, but he wouldn't come find us. He would simply stand at the top of the stairs and listen to our conversations or watch what we were doing. He was quite the little stinker.

After several weeks of this problem, we finally got him back to following directions by staying consistent. Once he realized we weren't backing down on the consequences, and we were on to his little ninja game, he eventually gave in.

Oh, how I wanted to quit and just give up the fight during this period of time. My husband and I were so frustrated with him. We had tried everything we could think of, but he still refused to follow the rules. It was becoming exhausting. During this situation, I clung to the scripture from James 1:2–4 that says, "Consider it pure joy, my brothers and sisters, whenever you face trials of many kinds, because you know that the testing of your faith produces perseverance. Let perseverance finish its work so that you may be mature and complete, not lacking anything" (NIV). There's that verse again! I struggled to find the joy in this situation, but I knew God was developing perseverance in me over this period of time.

I kept this verse in my mind and heart because I knew we needed to win this battle with Eli. We didn't need to win because this was such an important issue, although we did need our evenings to ourselves again, but we knew we had to win this smaller battle to show Eli to respect the rules of the house. Why is that so important at four years old? Because if you teach your kids to listen and obey from a young age, they are far more likely to listen and obey as they get older when the issues are more serious. If our boys see we don't really mean what we say when we give them rules, then when they are teenagers and we tell them drugs and alcohol are not acceptable, they likely won't listen. When we tell them premarital sex is not acceptable, they likely won't listen. When we tell them they have to maintain good grades to get into college, they likely won't listen. It all starts when they are young. Children are so smart. They learn and soak up every experience like sponges. Teach them to respect your rules, and stay consistent with them, even when you want to give in and let them win the battle.

It may not be perfect, but by having a consistent routine, your kids will likely be much more compliant with bedtime. And you will be a much happier parent getting to rest and recuperate your mind and body at the end of each day. Choose a bedtime, set up your routine, and stick with it even if your kids fight you at first. You are doing what is best for them, for you, and for your family.

Chapter 20

Surround Yourself with People Who Lift You Up

Walk with the wise and become wise; associate with
fools and get in trouble.—Proverbs 13:20 (NLT)

A few years ago, I was sitting at my church listening to a sermon from our pastor about having the right "they" in your life. I'll give you the *"Cliff's Notes"* version of the sermon. (I certainly hope I don't butcher it in case my pastor ever reads this book.) Our pastor was preaching about the friends and sometimes family members in your life who either build you up or tear you down. He gave the visual of a target. You are in the center of your target. Your closest friends and family should be in the inner circle with you, and everyone else belongs in the outermost circle. Our pastor used the example of Jesus. Jesus surrounded himself while here on earth with his disciples in the inner circle of his target, and everyone else, the people he healed, the people he helped, the people he preached to were all in the outer circle.

The main point of the sermon was to make sure you have the right "they" in your inner circle. Your inner circle should only be filled with people who build you up, not tear you down or take your energy away. These are the people who you rely on to give you clear biblical advice, to encourage you, and who offer you help when you need it. These people are also your most loyal and dear friends and family members whom you completely trust. Clearly Jesus had the right "they" in his inner circle with his disciples. Jesus' disciples helped him in his mission to spread God's Word throughout the world. He trusted his disciples to complete their task according to the will of his father. His disciples were also the people who came to his defense, particularly in the end when he was betrayed and the soldiers arrived to arrest Jesus. The Bible says Peter "had a sword, drew it and struck the high priest's servant, cutting off his right ear" (John 18:10 NIV). That's a good friend! That's someone I want in my inner circle. Jesus' disciples were people he trusted completely, and they were loyal to him and the purpose God had given him.

However, if you are familiar with the story of Judas, sometimes the wrong "they" will creep into your inner circle. Our pastor preached that when that happens, you cut these people out of your inner circle. You will almost never be able to pull someone up, but others can easily bring you down. It is *dangerous* to have close relationships with people who tear you down. Judas betrayed Jesus. The Bible says in Matthew 26: 14–16, "Then one of the twelve— the one called Judas Iscariot—went to the chief priests and asked, 'What are you willing to give me if I deliver him over to you?' So they counted out for him thirty pieces of silver. From then on Judas watched for an opportunity to hand him over" (NIV). The "him" in that passage is Jesus. Judas's betrayal of Jesus ultimately led to Jesus' death on the cross. Had Judas not been in Jesus' inner circle, he would never have been able to lead the soldiers to Jesus. He would not have known where Jesus would be hanging out. There would have been information he was not privy to had he not been part of the inner circle of Jesus.

Our pastor was very specific that you never have to force these people out of your life; simply remove them from your inner circle.

These people don't need full access to your life, and they certainly don't need to be trusted with things that are personal to you. Just as Jesus always associated with everyone, including sinners (remember, Jesus was called "a friend of sinners"), so should we. We are to be disciples to everyone and reach out to every single person we have the opportunity to, but we do not invite everyone into our inner circle. We'll never have the energy we need to be a good parent, friend, sister, etc., if we don't surround ourselves with people who build us up.

Why is this important as a parent? Several years ago, my husband and I had friends who were great people. We really enjoyed their company. We hung out with them a lot. They were new parents just like we were, so we naturally had a lot in common with them. We met this couple through our church, and they were even great Christian people. Since we spent a lot of time with them, we started to listen to their opinions on certain subjects. I won't go into specifics, as I would never want to embarrass these wonderful people. Sometimes I would disagree with their opinions, but I would listen anyway. After a while, I began to think there might be something to some of their ideas. So I began to voice some of their ideas and opinions on certain topics to my husband. He would listen as well, and eventually he started to believe some of the things they were telling us. The things they were saying were not bad things, they simply were not the things God wanted for our family.

Before we knew what had happened, our family was on a different track than we knew God was leading us to go. We were no longer attending our Bible study group that we had been in for years, and we were contemplating changing churches from the one we had known and loved for half a decade. By simply allowing these people to influence our family and our decisions, rather than trusting God to give us the clear direction he always gives, we were no longer walking in obedience to God. These people didn't ultimately cause us death, like Judas did to Jesus, but it did cause a lot of turmoil and a couple of rocky years in our marriage because we were not following the path God intended for us. In addition, this tremendously affected our parenting, since we were not in sync in our marriage. It caused inconsistency in the lives of our children regarding church. And ultimately, it was showing our children that attending Bible study was not important, and that being grounded and regularly attending our church was not a priority for our family. Had we allowed this friendship to continue as our children aged, and we continued to fall under the influence of this couple, the effect on our children could have been devastating.

I truly thank God for the convictions of my husband through that time in our lives. He could see very clearly after a while what was happening and took control of the situation. He moved our family back on track through a series of events and some other friends who continued to be strong examples in our lives.

When we came out on the other side and were back in our Bible study group and regularly attending our church again, I realized what had derailed us. Those friends were wonderful people, but they weren't a great influence on our family. I can't imagine where our family might be today without the influence of our Bible study group that we rejoined, without the children's ministry of our amazing church home that we went back to, and without the strong influence of some of the right "they" in our lives. So we made the very difficult decision to cut those great friends out of our inner circle. They are still friends, but we just don't count them as part of our inner circle who we spend the majority of our time with, and who we count on to help build us up. They are not the friends we run to when we need sound biblical advice or encouragement in our lives.

I have yet another example of this. I often need advice on parenting. I truly don't believe God intended for us to figure parenting out on our own. I believe he places people in our lives at specific times to help us through certain situations. There are some people I count as part of my inner circle of friends and family who are great at building me up, but I don't consider all of them experts at parenting. They have other strengths, gifts, and talents that I admire. However, there are very few people I ask for parenting advice. I believe when you ask for opinions from too many people, you often get confused about what the best idea might be. So when I had my first son, I chose my few "parenting experts" very carefully. I looked at their children to see how they behaved. I looked at how those parents treated their children. I looked at how consistent those parents were with their children, among many other things. Once I had found those "parenting experts" that I trusted to give me sound biblical advice, they were the only people I asked when I needed help. Those friends were the right "they" I needed in my life to help me when I was seeking parenting advice. I often think about it this way. I don't ask for financial advice from friends who are in debt. I don't ask for marriage advice from people who are divorced. So why would I ask for parenting advice from people I don't consider to be good biblical leaders when it comes to parenting? Make wise choices about who you ask when you need advice.

Surround yourself with the right "they" and remove the wrong "they" from your inner circle. I believe you will have a lot less confusion in your life about what to do, and you won't feel like you're being pulled in several different directions. And most importantly, you will be surrounded by life-giving people who provide you with the energy you need to be the best parent and person you can be.

Conclusion

My heart truly goes out to you, as parents. Parenting is the most difficult thing I have ever done in my life, and I've only just begun. I have no idea what's in store for me down the road, but I am assured that it will be difficult and filled with many trials and tribulations along the way.

If I can reiterate any one point from my life, it is that the only way to survive parenting is to rely on God for everything every single day. I don't know how I would make it through the daily struggles without having God there as my comforter, my peacemaker, my teacher, and my protector. He knows what is the very best for me, and when I rely on him and choose to be obedient to his Word, he directs my life and keeps me on the right path. I have no idea what my life would be like without God at the center. But I can guarantee it would not be filled with the overflowing blessings that he has poured into my life. The Bible says, "God can do anything, you know—far more than you could ever imagine or guess or request in your wildest dreams!" (Ephesians 3:20 MSG). I can promise you he has done far more than I could ever have imagined for my life. Give your life to God and see firsthand what he is capable of.

Something I've discovered over the years and even while writing this book is that I can't do it all. I sometimes think, *I can be a good wife today. And I can keep the house pretty clean today. But I did a really bad job with my kids.* Or, *I was an awesome, loving, and caring mom today. And my house was so clean when my husband got home. But now I have no energy left to be a good wife to him.* I've realized that I simply can't do it all, but what I can do is choose some of the things I know are important and do the best job I can to complete those. You don't have to do everything I suggest in this book every day. I sure don't! But I choose a couple of important things each day that I want to focus on, and I work toward being successful at those. Tomorrow I'll choose something else to focus on. I'll never be able to do it all every day, but I can do something to be a good mom every day. Just keep trying and stop beating yourself up over the things you are not able to do.

I hope my stories have been an encouragement to you on your journey of parenting. It is my prayer that these words, which God has placed on my heart through the writing of this book, will help you and guide you as you travel down this path. As I said in the beginning, I am no parenting expert. But God is, and I trust him to train me and teach me how to raise godly children. These are the lessons he has taught me along the way. My biggest desire in life is to raise children who love the Lord and who love others as they love themselves (paraphrased from Matthew 22:37–40). I pray the same for you and for your children. Trust God, pray to him every day, and read the Bible, and he will do the rest. God is so faithful.